## STUDIES IN ECONOMIC AND SOCIAL HISTORY

This series, specially commissioned by the Economic History Society, provides a guide to the current interpretations of the key themes of economic and social history in which advances have recently been made or in which there has been significant debate.

Originally entitled 'Studies in Economic History', in 1974 the series had its scope extended to include topics in social history, and the new series title, 'Studies in Economic and Social History', signalises this development.

The series gives readers access to the best work done, helps them to draw their own conclusions in major fields of study, and by means of the critical bibliography in each book guides them in the selection of further reading. The aim is to provide a springboard to further work rather than a set of pre-packaged conclusions or short-cuts.

## ECONOMIC HISTORY SOCIETY

The Economic History Society, which numbers over 3000 members, publishes the *Economic History Review* four times a year (free to members) and holds an annual conference. Enquiries about membership should be addressed to the Assistant Secretary, Economic History Society, Peterhouse, Cambridge. Full-time students may join at special rates.

# STUDIES IN ECONOMIC AND SOCIAL HISTORY

*Edited for the Economic History Society by T. C. Smout*

PUBLISHED

OTHER TITLES ARE IN PREPARATION

# Religion and the Working Class in Nineteenth-Century Britain

Prepared for
The Economic History Society by

## HUGH McLEOD

Department of Theology,
University of Birmingham

MACMILLAN

*First published 1984 by*
Higher and Further Education Division
MACMILLAN PUBLISHERS LTD
*London and Basingstoke*
*Companies and representatives*
*throughout the world*
*Printed in Hong Kong*

British Library Cataloguing in Publication Data
McLeod, Hugh
    Religion and the working class in nineteenth
    century Britain.—(Studies in economic and
    social history)
    1. Labor and laboring classes—Great Britain
    —History—19th century   2. Religion and
    society   3. Great Britain—Religious life
    and customs—History—19th century
    I. Title      II. Series
    306' .6' 0941      BL60
    ISBN 0-333-28115-2

# Contents

## Acknowledgements

I would like to thank Elizabeth Roberts, Paul Thompson and Thea Vigne for allowing me to quote from their oral history interviews.

## Note on References

References in the text within square brackets relate to the items listed alphabetically in sections I and II of the Select Bibliography, followed, where necessary, by the page numbers in italics; for example [R. Williams, 1958, *13*].

## Editor's Preface

SINCE 1968, when the Economic History Society and Macmillan published the first of the 'Studies in Economic and Social History', the series has established itself as a major teaching tool in universities, colleges and schools, and as a familiar landmark in serious bookshops throughout the country. A great deal of the credit for this must go to the wise leadership of its first editor, Professor M. W. Flinn, who retired at the end of 1977. The books tend to be bigger now than they were originally, and inevitably more expensive; but they have continued to provide information in modest compass at a reasonable price by the standards of modern academic publications.

There is no intention of departing from the principles of the first decade. Each book aims to survey findings and discussion in an important field of economic or social history that has been the subject of recent lively debate. It is meant as an introduction for readers who are not themselves professional researchers but who want to know what the discussion is all about – students, teachers and others generally interested in the subject. The authors, rather than either taking a strongly partisan line or suppressing their own critical faculties, set out the arguments and the problems as fairly as they can, and attempt a critical summary and explanation of them from their own judgement. The discipline now embraces so wide a field in the study of the human past that it would be inappropriate for each book to follow an identical plan, but all volumes will normally contain an extensive descriptive bibliography.

The series is not meant to provide all the answers but to help readers to see the problems clearly enough to form their own conclusions. We shall never agree in history, but the discipline will be well served if we know what we are disagreeing about, and why.

T. C. SMOUT

*Editor*

*University of St. Andrews*

# 1 Introduction

There seems to be almost complete disagreement among historians about the role and significance of religion in British working-class life during the nineteenth century. It is hardly surprising that the cultural and political consequences of religion have been vigorously debated; for many of the most important studies have been undertaken by historians with strong religious or political convictions whose work was at least partly motivated by an urgent concern with contemporary problems. E. R. Wickham, for instance, was moved to write by his experiences as an industrial chaplain, and his desire to improve the Church of England's missionary strategy. R. F. Wearmouth wrote as a loyal Methodist and adherent of the Labour Party, who wanted to vindicate the particular socialist tradition to which he belonged. Meanwhile, E. P. Thompson, a socialist of rather a different kind, has been at equal pains to discredit the interpretation of labour history of which Wearmouth has been the most assiduous exponent. Inevitably, in their framing of the questions, and in their selection and evaluation of the evidence, Christian and non-Christian, radical and conservative, Marxist and non-Marxist historians are going to differ: there are some questions to which there may never be agreed answers. More surprisingly there is no agreement on many questions of a more factual nature. Dogmatic assertions are indeed often made concerning the extent and distribution of working-class religious involvement, but one study contradicts another (consciously or not), and nothing approaching a consensus exists.

One reason for these confusions and uncertainties lies in the nature of the sources, which are often difficult to interpret and sometimes seem to lead in opposite directions. For instance, the censuses of church attendance are often quoted as evidence of widespread religious apathy; but apart from the problem of what constitutes a 'high' and what a 'low' attendance, it is unclear how far people's religious beliefs, or the influence of religion on their lives, can be inferred from the fact that they did or did not attend church on a given day. Religious apathy is also highlighted in a large part of the literature by middle-class or clerical observers of the working class; but here ignorance or prejudice often colours the picture. On the other hand, we have a large body of

9

nineteenth-century working-class autobiographies, quite a high proportion of which suggest that their authors were strongly interested in religion for at least part of their lives; but it would be unwise to generalise from the few individuals sufficiently articulate to have written their own life-story.

The only places we can hear the voices of a large spectrum of working-class people are the records of the home missionary societies and the tapes recorded by modern oral historians. Even here, there are major problems in the interpretation of this evidence, and once again these two kinds of source seem to point in opposite directions.

The domestic missionaries, who visited door to door in working-class neighbourhoods, had to keep diaries, in which they recorded the reception they met. They provided verbatim accounts of conversations they had, as well as much incidental information on such things as what the people were doing when they called. The diaries suggest a good deal of indifference and some hostility on the part of those visited, and they provide some support for the picture of a working class that had no time for religion. Nonetheless, the fact that missionaries concentrated on poorer and 'rougher' streets and courts means that the views of the more prosperous sections of the working class are likely to be under-represented. Moreover, many people saw the missionaries as 'intruders', as one Birmingham evangelist admitted [Carrs Lane MSS. vol. 61, entry for 4 December 1838], and they may have been more concerned with shutting them up and getting them out of the door than with a frank exposition of their own opinions.

In the last ten years or so a new major source for the history of the late nineteenth and early twentieth century has become available: taped interviews with large samples of old people who were brought up during that period. Two of the most ambitious projects have been those by Elizabeth Roberts, and by Paul Thompson and Thea Vigne [See Roberts, 1976; Thompson, 1977]. Roberts interviewed 170 people, who had been brought up in working-class families in three Lancashire towns; Thompson and Vigne co-ordinated interviews with some 500 people who in their social and regional origins were intended to be representative of the whole population of Great Britain as it was in 1911. Although religion was not among the principal subjects of investigation in either of these projects, most interviews included some discussion of religious beliefs and practices in the respondent's family. The evidence of both projects suggests that the church-going minority in the later Victorian working class was larger than is generally recognised, that more account needs to be taken of the influence of

Christianity on those who seldom went to church, and that the decline of the churches was a very long-drawn-out process. However, oral evidence may also contain important biases. For instance, oral history samples may over-represent the more prosperous and 'respectable' sections of the working class, both because more of them survive into old age, and because those who belong to organisations, or who have socially mobile children, may be more easily contacted by interviewers. In view of these contrasting kinds of bias in the major sources, it is important that any interpretation of working-class religion in the nineteenth century should be based on the widest possible range of evidence.

The two writers who did most to revive interest in the history of English working-class religion were Wickham [1957] and Inglis [1963]. Wickham, as founder of the Sheffield Industrial Mission, wanted to investigate the historical roots of present-day religious apathy. Echoing an earlier Anglican bishop, who wrote in 1896, 'It is not that the Church of God has lost the great towns, it has never had them', Wickham traced the non-church-going habits of the Sheffield working class back to the eighteenth century. From the 1820s, Wickham showed, most denominations were building churches in working-class areas, and there was at least an awareness of the resentment caused by the prevalence of class distinctions within the church; but most of the working class still remained aloof. Inglis took working-class alienation from the churches more or less for granted. His main interest was in attempts by the churches to respond with new organisations, new methods of evangelism, and a more vigorous concern with social reform. His conclusion was that such efforts were bound to fail as long as the churches remained fundamentally committed to the capitalist system.

In the 1970s there were signs of dissatisfaction with the rather negative treatment of working-class religion by Wickham and Inglis, and their readiness to accept middle-class definitions of religiosity, such as regular church attendance. It was argued that the working class had their own different, but equally valid approach to religion, which was strongly practical, and was concerned especially with mutual aid, and with maintaining standards of 'decent' behaviour [McLeod, 1974; Ainsworth, 1977]. But the prevailing view, enshrined in most textbooks, is based on Wickham and Inglis, and stresses the 'apathy' or 'indifference' of the English working class to religion. Meacham [1977], in an interesting reassessment of working-class life at the end of the century, which emphasises relationships with neighbours and kin, even manages to dispose of religion in a single paragraph.

The most influential study of Scottish religion has been MacLaren's book on Aberdeen [1974]. This was mainly concerned with the relationship between the great Disruption of the Scottish church in 1843 and the development of the middle class. MacLaren argued that the conflict between the 'Old Kirk' and the 'Free Kirk' reflected the conflict between the well-established and the newly rich sections of the urban élite. But he went on to argue that both churches neglected the interests of their working-class members. He implied that the result was the alienation of the latter from the Presbyterian churches. This view seems to be accepted by the authors of the standard church history of eighteenth- and nineteenth-century Scotland [Drummond and Bulloch, 1978, 143-8], though they suggest that Presbyterianism had a much bigger following among the 'decent working class' than among the 'poor and destitute'. The one major exception to this apparent alienation from organised religion that is generally accepted by English and Scottish historians is the Irish immigrant population [Gilbert, 1976, 45-7; Drummond and Bulloch, 1978, 147-8].

However, the general view is that Wales was different. The most substantial study of working-class religion in industrial south Wales [Davies, 1965] does indeed end with the conquest of the chapels by the shopkeepers and the colliery managers. But this, and the consequent alienation of many miners and factory workers, only came in the last years of the nineteenth century, and the first part of the twentieth. For most of the nineteenth century, Davies argues, the chapels were mainly working-class in membership, and exercised an immense influence on working-class life in the industrial valleys. In spite of important criticisms of the details of Davies' argument [Evans, 1977], no-one has yet challenged this broad outline [cf. Lambert, 1976].

In Scotland there is a body of pamphlets and published sermons going back at least to the 1750s which complains of the poor state of religion, and especially of low church attendance; but it seems to have been only in the 1830s that the urban working class were identified as the main body of absentees [Withrington, 1970]. Wickham suggests that it was also in the 1830s that the English middle class became generally aware that a large part of the working class did not attend church – though certainly many individual clergymen had been commenting on this fact for many years before that. The desire to publicise this situation, and to suggest possible remedies, gave rise to an equally large literature on working-class irreligion in England. At first sight it presents irrefutable support for the picture of general religious apathy suggested by authors such as Inglis and Meacham.

However, the situation becomes more complicated when we look in greater detail at the counts of church attendance and at church membership records.

To begin with the religious censuses, conducted nationally in 1851, and in various localities in 1881: these show big regional variations in the level of church-going, and considerable local variation within some regions. In England the regions of high church-going were the east midlands and the south-west, where attendances were high both in town and country, though usually higher in the country. Most of the major cities were outside these regions, but in 1851 Bristol, Plymouth, Leicester and Nottingham all reported attendances above the urban average [McLeod, 1973]. In some small industrial communities attendances were higher still. For instance, several of the mining and nailing villages in the Black Country had well over 60 per cent in 1851, though attendance patterns varied greatly within a small area [Robson, 1979]. In Wales church-going in both town and country was well above the English average, and in 1851 Merthyr Tydfil, then the largest town in Wales, had a higher percentage of church-goers than any English town but Colchester. The Scottish figures have so far been subjected to less analysis, but the present view is that Scottish church-going was slightly higher than English. Rural attendance varied very widely, while urban attendance varied more narrowly and was clearly higher than the English average. [Brown, 1981, *I, 199-206*].

Where comparison between middle-class and working-class areas of cities is possible, the former nearly always show higher levels of church attendance and membership. The only exception appears to be Liverpool, where church-going was low in Protestant working-class districts but exceeded suburban levels in some Catholic working-class areas. However, it is clear that both working-class and middle-class levels of church-going were affected by regional differences. For instance, in the 1880s, attendance at all churches was 15–20 per cent in working-class areas, and about 40 per cent in middle-class suburbs of London and Birmingham, which were near the bottom of the scale of urban church-going; but in Bristol, which was near the top, it was 40 per cent in working-class areas, and 66 per cent in a wealthy suburb [McLeod, 1973].

However, church attendance censuses have their limitations, as indicators even of who went to church, let alone of anything else. For instance, there is no way of knowing what proportion of regular attenders were absent on the day of the census; and the censuses can give no precise indication of the social composition of congregations. Oral history suggests that the percentage of working-class people attending church fairly regularly was higher than is generally recognised. Here I have used Thompson and Vigne's interviews with men and women born in Britain between 1872 and 1906. About 40 per cent of respondents brought up in working-class families in industrial districts of England reported that when they were young their mother was a regular church-goer; the proportion was a good deal lower (24 per cent) in London, but much higher in Wales and Scotland. The proportion of fathers who were regular attenders was around 20 per cent in London, the Potteries, the north midlands and the north-east; but 32 per cent in Lancashire, 40 per cent in Yorkshire, and over 50 per cent in Wales and Scotland.

Research in church membership records tends to show quite high proportions of working-class members in many congregations. A large-scale analysis of Nonconformist registers of baptisms and burials, mainly from the period 1800–37 [Gilbert, 1976], suggested that artisans were by far the largest occupational group, and that these, together with smaller numbers of labourers and miners, made up about 75 per cent of the Methodists, Baptists and Congregationalists whose occupations were recorded in the registers. Admittedly, the frequent vagueness of occupational descriptions sometimes makes it hard to distinguish between employer, employee and self-employed. But Gilbert concludes that the great expansion of English Nonconformity between about 1780 and 1840 was mainly due to recruitment among the working class, though these denominations were becoming more middle class in the mid-nineteenth century. However, a comprehensive survey by Field [1977] of local studies of Methodist membership suggests that the pattern described by Gilbert persisted much longer, and that it is only in the twentieth century that Methodism has become predominantly middle class. Phillips [1982, *14, 79, 169, 176*] analysed marriage and baptismal registers from Wesleyan, Primitive, Baptist and Congregationalist chapels in Lancashire cotton towns during the period 1830–70. Most showed a preponderance of working-class occupations; even a membership list from Bolton's leading Unitarian chapel showed a significant minority of working-class members [see also Foster, 1974, *215*]. Meanwhile, Hillis [1981, *54–5*] has argued on the basis of baptismal records that the members of Glasgow Presbyterian churches between 1845 and 1865 were predominantly working class – though it is clear that the proportion of working-class members in the non-established churches (54 per

14

cent) was considerably less than in the population as a whole. All these writers would concede that middle-class church members were heavily over-represented in positions of leadership. It is also obvious that there were considerable differences between the various congregations of the same denomination, the prestige 'West End' chapel, for instance, having little in common with the back-street 'Little Bethel'. Nonetheless, the impact of this new research has so far been very limited. The prevailing view of Victorian working-class religion is still largely derived from Wickham, Inglis and MacLaren.

The picture becomes even more confused when we look at the large body of literature which has attempted to gauge the influence of religion on working-class politics and on more general cultural changes. There has been intense, and sometimes bitter, conflict between proponents of different theories as to the nature of this influence. But most of the contributors to these debates have agreed that religion was an important factor. Some historians, in making this assumption, have simply ignored the evidence of mass religious indifference. More recently, general familiarity with the work of writers like Inglis has forced political historians to recognise that they have a problem on their hands. One solution has been to suggest that religion was important because of its influence on a powerful minority within the working class, for instance the labour aristocracy [Foster, 1974]. Another has been to suggest that religion was temporarily important in certain strategic areas of the country in the early years of the century, but that it then declined – this seems to be the view of Thompson [1968] and Gilbert [1976]. However, historians of the middle and later Victorian years have had to recognise the fact that religion continued to be an important factor in politics. So Joyce [1980] and Ainsworth [1977] have argued that religious loyalties exercised a major influence on Lancashire working-class politics, and that they cannot be adequately measured by counting attendance at services.

In this they are certainly right (though the evidence collected by Roberts and by Thompson and Vigne suggests that formal church-going was somewhat higher than they allow). Christianity and the Christian churches had a pervasive influence in nineteenth-century British society, which was spread very widely, even if sometimes rather thinly. Children whose parents seldom attended church still learnt prayers at their mother's knee, heard grace said at meals, sang hymns with their parents, went to Sunday School, and very often to a denominational day school. The poorer working-class children grew up with a good knowledge of the places where free breakfasts could be found, which usually meant a mission-hall of one kind or another; as teenagers they would often belong to a church-sponsored club – boxing was an Anglican speciality, and many famous football teams, most notably Aston Villa in England and Celtic in Scotland, have church origins (Methodist and Catholic respectively); when they began to look for work, they would find that many employers had associations with a particular religious denomination, and expected their employees to share this association [Cox, 1982, *48-105*; MacLaren, 1974, *144-66*; Roberts, 1976, *62-4*; Joyce, 1980, *176-7*].

It is also worth noting that many non-church-goers had been through phases of active church involvement. As one example, it is well known that the mass conversions achieved by Methodist preachers in the early nineteenth century were often followed by widespread backsliding. However, it does not follow that lapsed Methodists necessarily ceased to hold Methodist beliefs or, indeed, in their own eyes to remain Methodists. In fact, a Calvinist missionary who went from door to door in Birmingham in the 1830s claimed that the city was full of lapsed Methodists, and that the prevalence of Methodist ideas was a major reason for the poor response to his own efforts [Robson, 1978].

The history of nineteenth-century working-class religion is many-sided. Any interpretation that does anything like justice to the subject must take account of opposing tendencies: of the secularising trends, and also of the continuing strengths of working-class religion; of the influential secularist minority, and also of the majority who retained some kind of link with their churches; of churches that were middle-class controlled, and those that were products of working-class self-help; of radical, conservative, and quietist interpretations of Christianity.

# 2  The 1790s

The eighteenth century saw a gradual weakening of the influence of the Established Church, both in England and in Scotland. In the educated classes the prevailing style of religion tended to become rational, moralistic and cautious; the emotional temperature was low, and the level of commitment required was fairly low too. Scepticism and indifference were also widespread. Those who looked for more democratic and more emotionally satisfying forms of religion were leaving the parish churches to form their own prayer groups, and sometimes their separate places of worship. In Scotland, the catalyst was the Patronage Act of 1712, confirming the rights of patrons to nominate parish ministers, even in defiance of the wishes of the congregation. The Secession of 1733 started a steady trickle of defections from the Kirk; the numerous breakaway churches formed between the mid-eighteenth century and the mid-nineteenth were mostly Calvinist in theology and church government, but hostile to the precise form that Calvinism took in the Established Church of Scotland. In England several varieties of Protestant Dissent had survived from the seventeenth century. After a period of decline, they were gradually growing again by the 1740s. That same decade saw the beginnings of Methodism. The societies set up by John Wesley, an Anglican clergyman, were intended to revive the Church of England; but the Methodists were generally repudiated by the bishops and parish clergy, who suspected their fanaticism and their lack of respect for authority. Before long Methodists effectively formed a separate religious community.

At the same time, the building of new churches failed to keep pace with the growth of population, especially in cities and in the centres of domestic industry. As early as 1736 in Sheffield, and 1751 in Leeds, the clergy had been complaining that the lack of churches encouraged the spread of Nonconformity and non-church-going. Many Lancashire incumbents said the same in 1778 [Greaves, 1968, *54, 84*; Chester Diocesan Articles of Enquiry]. Completely new communities were growing up in the mining, ironworking and textile districts of northern England, central Scotland and south Wales, often several miles from the nearest parish church. The weakness of the Established

17

Churches left a religious vacuum which was only sometimes filled by Nonconformity or by militant secularism. Two small industrial towns, lying a few miles east of Manchester, can be taken to illustrate the possibilities. Dukinfield had about 10,000 people when the first Anglican church was built in 1841; Droylesden had 6000 when the Anglicans arrived in 1848. By the former date, Dukinfield had no less than seventeen Nonconformist chapels. However, in Droylesden, where several decades of Methodist activity had evoked little response, a survey of 1845 reported that only 45 out of 450 families questioned were Methodist, while 355 belonged to no church at all [Rose, n.d., 18]. So in some of the new industrial communities of the later eighteenth and early nineteenth centuries, patterns of life were developing in which the church had little part.

However, the events of 1789 and the years immediately following added an explosive political ingredient to the religious mixture. The first to welcome the revolution in France were middle-class Dissenters. But in 1791 the reforming movement began to broaden. First in Sheffield, then in London, Norwich and many other towns, artisans began to organise, demanding a comprehensive reform of Parliament and the vote for all adult males. Tom Paine's *Rights of Man* became their sacred text. The authorities reacted to the radical threat by banning public meetings, closing newspapers, dissolving organisations and putting their leaders in prison. By the end of the 1790s, the conservative forces appeared to have won; but the basis for a lasting split in British society had been laid. Meanwhile the Established Church, both in England and Scotland, rallied to the defence of the old order. Sermons extolling monarchy and condemning democracy became part of the standard fare in the parish churches.

Instead of the gradual decline of the Established Churches, which had been going on for some time, there now came a period of polarisation. There was a great revival of interest in established religion in the upper and upper middle classes. Conservatives saw the Established Churches, with their nationwide network of parishes, as vital agencies for the preservation of a paternalistic, hierarchical society. On the other hand, the conservatism which became so predominant in the Established Churches discredited them in the eyes of all those who wanted political reform. The 1790s saw a great acceleration in the growth of Nonconformist religion; this growth continued for several decades, and the Dissenting churches were among the most important institutions in nineteenth-century British society. And at a time of social and political upheaval unequalled since the mid-seventeenth century, millenarianism evoked a widespread, though less permanent interest. It was also in this decade that a significant minority of the working class began to reject Christianity altogether. Each of these movements, in its own way, reflected the hopes of those who believed that the fall of the French monarchy and the apparently impending demise of the papacy heralded a new era of equality and social justice. Nor was there any sharp demarcation between those who expected the impending revolution to be the work of God, and those who saw it as a purely human task. Political activists were often interested in prophecies [Harrison, 1979, *223-6*; J. Hopkins, 1982, *149-69*]; equally, many church reformers were also political reformers – for instance the Methodist New Connexion, which broke away from the Wesleyans in 1797, became known as the 'Tom Paine Methodists' [E. P. Thompson, 1968, *48-9*]

The first of the prophets to attract widespread attention in the revolutionary years was Richard Brothers, a naval officer living in London. In 1795 the government had him interrogated with a view to treason charges, but decided instead to incarcerate him in a lunatic asylum. However, from 1801 until her death in 1814, Joanna Southcott enjoyed a following probably unequalled by any other millenarian prophet in English history. As did Brothers, she built her initial reputation on her ability to foretell the revolutions, wars, harvest failures, which occurred with such frequency in the 1790s. The nationwide interest in her published prophecies arose from the belief that the cataclysmic events of those years had a place in God's plan for the salvation of mankind, and that the millennial kingdom was coming soon. Her writings offered interpretations of the prophetic books of the Bible, predictions derived from dreams and visions, social criticism, and pictures of a glorious future. She came from a long tradition of Protestant millenarians who hoped to see into the future with the aid of Daniel and Revelation. Disruptive social change at home and spectacular political upheavals in Europe gave fresh urgency to these old puzzles. Not surprisingly, Southcottians were numerous in fast-growing industrial towns like Ashton-under-Lyne, and in many parts of the West Riding. But the most striking point is the breadth of her appeal: there were also thousands of 'Johannas' in London, and the densest concentration seems to have been in the villages and small towns of her native West Country [J. Hopkins, 1982, *75-85*].

While the millenarians were giving new life to a very old tradition, the organised irreligion of the 1790s was a new phenomenon. A crucial influence was Tom Paine's *Age of Reason*, published in 1794 [Royle,

1974, *23-31*]. This included a critique of the Bible from a deist point of view. That is, Paine believed in a Supreme Being, but rejected all specifically Christian doctrines, and all of the Christian churches. Paine's book carried with it the authority of the writer of *The Rights of Man*, though its popularity was narrower. For instance, the London Corresponding Society decided to publish *The Age of Reason*, but many members resigned in protest. In London, at least, the 'infidels' seem to have won a lot of support among radicals in the 1790s. From 1795 onwards infidel societies were being formed, usually meeting to hear lectures in public-house club rooms on Wednesday and Sunday evenings. Until 1798, when the magistrates began to suppress their activities, infidel speakers joined the many varieties of religious propagandists who already made Sunday a great day for open-air preaching. Paine's method of attacking Christianity – an assault on the credibility of the Bible – was indeed well-suited to the task of undermining the faith of a nation of Bible-reading Protestants, especially since his extremely literalist approach to the task of finding inconsistencies and absurdities in the sacred text closely paralleled the approach of many devout believers. But the chief appeal of the infidel gospel was probably that indicated by a contemporary critic, who noted [W. H. Reid, *The Rise and Dissolution of the Infidel Societies of the Metropolis*, 1800] that among members of the radical societies 'the bare circumstance of having the Age of Reason in a house was deemed a collateral proof of the *civism* of the possessor'. The infidels were men who had burned the bridges linking them with the respectable society of their day; their only home was the beleaguered radical subculture, and the totality of their commitment could for that reason be the more readily believed.

The spread of infidelity in the north-western textile district can be traced in the replies of clergy to the visitation queries sent by the Bishop of Chester. In 1778 and 1789 not a single clergyman in the Deanery of Manchester reported the presence of more than a handful of unbelievers in his parish, though many of them mentioned large numbers of non-church-goers. A typical comment was that from Radcliffe in 1789: 'There are none who profess to disregard Religion, but many of the poorer sort are hindered (partly by family concerns, partly by want to decent clothing) from attending the public worship of God on the Lord's Day.' But the next visitation, in 1804, revealed a new factor in the situation. The incumbent of Pendleton noted that the number of non-church-goers had increased 'since revolutionary principles became so prevalent', and the reply from Mottram stated:

'Some disbelieve the Scriptures and others have no religion in them. These persons work in the woollen and cotton trades.' Further north, in Colne, the incumbent blamed the increase in non-church-going on 'the execrable writings of the infamous Paine', who was also named in neighbouring Bacup, though his following was said to be limited to a 'few ignorant Deists'. However, the incumbent of St George's, Bolton, reckoned that several thousand people in that town had been influenced by infidelity. In 1811, the number of clergy mentioning the spread of infidelity dropped slightly, but two Oldham clergymen stated that infidel beliefs, such as the denial of immortality, were common [Chester Diocesan Articles of Enquiry].

But where thousands were attracted to the new infidel societies, hundreds of thousands were being drawn to hear Nonconformist itinerant preachers, or to join chapels and cottage meetings. In England, the number of new licences for permanent places of worship increased from 251 in the 1780s to 832 in the 1790s; licences for temporary places of worship rose from 1154 to 3413 [Gilbert, 1976, 34]. Typical of the areas where Dissent was booming was the West Riding of Yorkshire, centre of a fast-growing woollen industry and also of political radicalism, where licences for temporary places of Dissenting worship rose from 73 in the 1780s to 401 in the 1790s [Wallace, 1975, 431]. The rapid growth of Nonconformity continued throughout the first half of the nineteenth century. Between 1791 and 1851 the population of England approximately doubled. But the number of Methodists increased by nine times; Gilbert estimates that the number of Independents (Congregationalists) increased by six times, and the Baptists by seven times [Gilbert, 1976, 31, 37]. In south Wales, where the growth of Nonconformity in the nineteenth century was even more spectacular, the period of rapid growth seems to have begun slightly later, after about 1800 [Davies, 1965, 15]. In Scotland, too, the growth of Dissent accelerated in the 1790s, though the change of pace was much less marked than it was south of the border; the basic pattern is of a fairly steady and continuous increase in the number of Dissenting congregations from the 1730s to the 1830s [W. MacKelvie, *Annals and Statistics of the United Presbyterian Church,* Edinburgh, 1873]. The major new development in the 1790s was the lay-preaching movement led by the Haldane brothers, which aroused great anxiety among conservative ministers, and laid the basis for the Scottish Congregational and Baptist churches. However, these remained much smaller than in England or Wales.

As already mentioned, the present view among historians of English

Nonconformity is that the chapels recruited predominantly from the working class during their period of rapid expansion. The same seems to be true of the chapels in south Wales [Davies, 1965, *18*; Evans. 1977, Chapter 2]. The social composition of Scottish Dissent in the later eighteenth and early nineteenth century has not been the subject of any detailed research. MacLaren [1974, *27*] states that Dissenters were drawn from 'shopkeepers', 'tradesmen' and 'the artisans and peasantry'.

Historians have generally agreed that the remarkable development of Nonconformity during this period was related to the growth of industry, migration to cities and industrial villages, and the intensification of class antagonisms that was associated with the decline of paternalism. But there is no agreement as to what the relationship between social and religious change was. It is common ground that chapels sprang up where the Established Churches were weak: in new communities without their own parish church, in outlying hamlets, in working-class neighbourhoods of cities. It is evident that groups such as the Methodists were filling a vacuum left by the failure of the Established Churches; but it is not evident why those neglected by the parish church should have chosen to spend their free time at Methodist meetings, rather than, for instance, at a pub, or at secularist lectures. Similarly, it is generally agreed that Nonconformist chapels had very important functions as community centres in newly developing districts, with large immigrant populations. But again, this explanation begs the question of why it was specifically Nonconformity that met their needs. There have been two quite different ways of answering this question. One has been to follow the lead provided in the 1840s by Karl Marx, who stated that: 'Religion is the heart of a heartless world, just as it is the spirit of spiritless conditions. It is the opium of the people.' According to this view, argued most powerfully by E. P. Thompson [1968], religion was most attractive to the people at times when the apparent hopelessness of their earthly condition encouraged them to seek an other-worldly solution to their problems; at the same time, religion tended to divert working-class energies away from the tasks of political and trade union organisation, and for this reason it was often promoted by employers. According to the contrary view, 'Evangelical Nonconformity echoed the *aspirations* rather than the *despair* of the working classes' [Gilbert, 1976, *83*].

In Thompson's view [1968, *385-411*] the crucial importance of Methodism lay in the fact that it was used by employers to train the first and second generations of factory workers in habits of discipline, regularity and obedience. It made the worker 'his own slave-driver'. But this raises the question of why such a doctrine was enthusiastically accepted by many working-class people. Thompson has several answers: adult Methodists were often the end-result of effective indoctrination of the young in the Sunday Schools that were established in large numbers from about 1780; Methodism 'did offer to the uprooted and abandoned people of the Industrial Revolution some kind of community to replace the older community patterns which were being displaced'; and, above all, the many political defeats suffered by working-class radicals in the 1790s and in the following decades created moods of temporary desperation, in which the religious revivalist could bring about mass conversions [E. P. Thompson, 1968, *411-40*; see also Baxter, 1974]. E. T. Davies [1965, *17-18, 49*] explains the great growth of Nonconformity in industrial south Wales in somewhat similar terms. He suggests that the chapels were especially attractive to immigrants from the countryside, seeking some tenuous link with home. Above all, he stresses the drab surroundings, narrow horizons and impoverished culture of the Industrial Revolution working-class community: 'many went to chapel in those days because there was nowhere else to go'.

The alternative view sees the chapels not as compensations for the failure of radical politics, but as an integral part of the same movement of self-assertion by people from the working and lower middle classes. Hobsbawm [1964, *29*] noted that strongholds of Methodism were often strongholds of radicalism (e.g. Bradford and Huddersfield). His explanation was [*32-3*] that working-class evangelicalism had many of the same causes as popular radicalism, and often appealed to the same people. Laqueur advanced similar arguments in his study of the Sunday School movement [1976]. As against the view which sees Sunday Schools mainly as agencies of ruling class indoctrination of the masses, Laqueur argued that the main reason Sunday Schools flourished was that working-class parents wanted the education they provided, and generally endorsed the values that they taught. He stressed the affinities between working-class Sunday School teachers and radical activists: both had their roots in the emerging 'respectable' working-class culture, which tended to be fascinated by the printed page, hostile to many traditional amusements, orderly, self-respecting and politically aware.

This line of argument has been most fully developed by Gilbert [1976]. In an impressively coherent interpretation of the rise and decline of English Nonconformity from the eighteenth century to the twentieth, he suggested that working-class chapels were especially characteristic of the early stages of the Industrial Revolution. He argued that they were strongest in the industrial village, which he saw as a transitional kind of community between the mainly Anglican countryside and the religiously apathetic cities; he suggested that the typical working-class Nonconformist was not a factory worker, but a handloom weaver or some other kind of domestic worker. In a hierarchical and privilege-ridden society, where much of the rural population lived under the thumb of squire and parson, Nonconformity expressed and legitimated the independence of the craftsmen and domestic workers. It provided opportunities for status and responsibility as preachers, class leaders or Sunday School teachers; the puritanism of the Nonconformists, and their encouragement of hard work, self-discipline, literacy and a generally methodical approach to life, provided a formula for family survival and even modest prosperity, as well as a basis for pride in the face of social 'superiors'. In support of his view that popular evangelicalism was a fruit of hope rather than of despair, Gilbert notes [1976, *66, 83*] that Nonconformity in the later eighteenth and early nineteenth centuries appealed much more strongly to artisans than to the poorest sections of the working-class.

This is one of the strongest arguments in favour of Gilbert's interpretation, and by the later nineteenth century there is clear evidence from London, and hints from elsewhere, that the chapels recruited much more often among the skilled than the unskilled working class, and that extreme poverty tended to produce apathy and bitterness rather than religious conversion [McLeod, 1974, *54, 283, 309*; Field, 1977, *206-10*; Wickham, 1957, *131-6*]. However, evidence for the late eighteenth and early nineteenth centuries is scantier. A study of later eighteenth-century Yorkshire, which included an occupational analysis of registers from many chapels, largely confirmed Gilbert's picture: artisans were the largest occupational group, and labourers were under-represented [Wallace, 1975, *206-8, 216, 240-8*]. On the other hand, research on the strongly Methodist Black Country suggests that Gilbert's category of 'artisan' is too broad and imprecise: Gilbert was right to suggest that nailers were the mainstay of Black Country chapels, but wrong to describe this essentially unskilled group as artisans [E. Hopkins, 1983]. Clearly, much more detailed local research is needed before any definite conclusions can be drawn.

Of course there is no reason why any one kind of interpretation of the popular evangelical movements of these years should be regarded as definitive. In reality, most movements (and most individuals) contain contradictory elements within them. While many studies have suffered from overstatement of their author's case [e.g. Wearmouth, 1937; Stigant, 1971], the most convincing interpretations have been those that have stressed the complexities and ambiguities of these movements. Thompson, in particular, has emphasised the many-sided and continually changing character of Methodism during the years 1790–1830. The attractions of evangelicalism obviously varied over time, and they may have varied between different kinds of community; it is also necessary to ask not only why many people were converted in periods of revival, but also who remained in the chapel and why, while many of their colleagues soon became backsliders. Despair or acute anxiety, caused by natural disasters such as cholera epidemics [see Robson, 1979], or by political disasters, may often have precipitated periods of mass conversion. But many such conversions were short-lived. The kind of framework of interpretation provided by Gilbert is more helpful in explaining why some of the converts stayed on, becoming lifelong chapel-goers, and why chapels remained important institutions in working-class communities across several generations. In such an explanation, a very wide range of factors needs to be considered. One of the strengths of Gilbert's argument is that he gives due weight both to the political implications of evangelical movements, and to the message of individual salvation which was the primary concern of the evangelists; to the community life provided by the chapels, and to the models for day-to-day living that the chapel provided. He could, however, have gone further in placing evangelicalism within the context of existing folk-beliefs, religious traditions, codes of behaviour – showing how the chapels reflected certain aspects of the popular culture of their time, while challenging others. [See the discussion of the relationship between Methodism and popular 'superstition' in Rule, 1971, *240-60*; also Lawson, 1887, 50.] In this respect, no account of urban and industrial evangelicalism in the early nineteenth century quite matches the richness of Obelkevich's study [1976] of Methodism and of 'popular religion' in rural Lincolnshire.

## 3  From Magic to Moralism

On a wet Sunday morning in May 1807, several thousand people gathered on the top of Mow Cop, an isolated hill on the borders of Cheshire and Staffordshire. They had come for a day of praying, preaching, hymn-singing and testimonies. Such 'Camp Meetings' were a well-established feature of religious life on the American frontier, where they would last several days. The Wesleyan Conference decided that meetings of this sort were not desirable in England, where they seemed an obstacle to the church discipline and ministerial control that were increasingly preoccupying the Wesleyan leadership. As a result, the leaders of the Staffordshire revival, a carpenter named Hugh Bourne and a potter, William Clowes, were expelled from the Wesleyan Connexion. They subsequently joined with the 'Magic Methodists' of Delamere Forest in Cheshire, one of several groups living at this time on the margins of official Methodism. In 1812 they assumed the title of 'Primitive Methodists'. At first they grew fast, and by the end of the century they had 200,000 members. They were seen at the time, and historians have since generally agreed they were, as the most thoroughly working class of major religious denominations in nineteenth-century England. Many of the trends in working-class religion during that century are epitomised in their history.

Early Primitive Methodists had one over-riding concern: to bring the gospel of salvation through faith in Jesus Christ to as many sinners as possible. They believed that everyone was a sinner, but that everyone could be saved, if they repented of their sins and accepted God's offer of forgiveness. They had an infallible guide in all areas of life in the Bible, which they regarded as the Word of God, inspired as a whole and in every detail. It was desperately important to them that the preaching of the gospel should take priority over everything else, for those who repented and believed would be rewarded with everlasting life, but those who remained in their sins would suffer eternal punishment. In these respects, they belonged to a tradition of fundamentalist evangelical Protestantism, which goes back to the Reformation and continues to the present day (though its main strongholds are now in the United States). But in many other ways they were essentially men and women of their own time, rooted in the mental world and the rapidly changing society of early nineteenth-century England.

First, they were great dreamers. Like the early Anabaptists and Quakers, or present-day Pentecostalists, but quite unlike most Lutherans, Calvinists or Anglicans, they believed that God speaks directly to men through dreams and visions. This was obviously an attractive doctrine for the poor, for here was a form of religious experience that was as accessible to a completely illiterate person as to the greatest theologian or biblical scholar. In practice, Primitive Methodists read their Bibles as often as they could, and took the general principles of their faith and practice from there. But when it came to specific problems about which the Bible offered no clear guidance, they took advantage of direct inspiration. The early Primitive Methodists were also close to the world of popular magic. As Valenze says [1982, 146-7], there was a thin line between the 'female saint' and the 'wise woman'. Elizabeth Russell, a leading figure in the Primitive Methodist evangelisation of the Wiltshire/Berkshire borders in the 1820s and 1830s, was credited with healing powers, and was sometimes sought out by those who believed she could tell fortunes. The 'Ranters', as the Primitives were popularly termed in their early days, shared all the beliefs in witches, boggards, physical mani-festations of the Devil, miraculous healings and special providences that were widespread in the countryside and the industrial villages of early nineteenth-century England [Obelkevich, 1976; Lawson, 1887, 48-53], and probably in the cities too, though much less is known about urban folklore [but see Lees, 1979, 185-9]. They put these generally held beliefs into a framework of evangelical religion, in terms of which the world was no longer a chaos of random supernatural interventions, but a battlefield, where God and the Devil fought for the soul of each individual human being. When seen in this light, the most apparently insignificant events of everyday life took on great importance, and the most humdrum life acquired infinite meaning. Nor was there any Calvinist elect: God called everyone to fight on his side by spreading the gospel and living a Christian life.

So the main concern of the Primitive pioneers was all-out evangelism, and no tradition, convention or law was allowed to stand in the way. No educational qualifications were required of their early preachers, neither was there any minimum age. The point that caused most controversy at the time was that many of their early preachers were women. The Anglican church and the Calvinistic branches of

Dissent saw preaching as an office to which only men were called. The Wesleyans had a number of women preachers, but the practice was condemned by Conference in 1803. Only the Quakers had an unbroken tradition of preaching by women. As long as evangelism remained the over-riding priority, and as long as Primitive Methodism existed on the margins of respectable society, they made no distinction between the sexes in preaching, though organisational matters seem always to have been a male preserve.

Their determination that nothing should stand in the way of the preaching of the gospel meant that the early Primitives were rebels, whether or not they wished it. Primitive Methodism began with deliberate defiance of the Wesleyan Conference. For many years after, their right to preach was constantly challenged by magistrates, or by mob violence. Periods in prison for vagrancy or for obstructing the highway were part of the standard experience of the early preachers. According to Kendall [1902, 96], the persecution was worst in the south, where 'the Church, as by law established, had for long had its own way, unchecked and unthwarted by "schism"', and clergy and magistrates were determined it should stay that way. The early leaders of the sect were not interested in politics. In any case, they feared that if Primitive Methodists became known as active radicals, the government might try to suppress their evangelistic activity [Wearmouth, 1937, 170]. But at the local level, 'Ranters' shared the sufferings and the hopes of their working-class neighbours, and the rebelliousness that was implicit in being a Primitive Methodist often made 'Ranter' preachers natural leaders of their own communities in political and trade union activity. For instance, in the strikes on the north-east coalfield in the 1830s and 1840s, the miners' leaders seem mainly to have been Primitive Methodists. They saw the owners in much the same light that Methodist evangelists saw persecuting magistrates and clergymen: they were paper tigers, who looked fearsome, but could not withstand the power of the truth. 'Ranters' rejoiced at the divine punishments suffered by blacklegs, much as they rejoiced at the accidents that frequently befell notorious persecutors. God was on their side, whether it was in the preaching of the gospel, or in the struggle for justice, and he often used rather rough tactics. In both instances, however, it was for God, not man, to punish. The saint should stand his ground, refuse to be intimidated, insist on his rights, but not attempt violence of any kind [Colls, 1977, 97-116; Wearmouth, 1937, 183-91; Kent, 1978, 40-2].

Primitive Methodism also had important implications for the self-image and codes of behaviour of the miners, farm labourers, nailers and domestic servants whom the movement attracted. It offered them a formula for self-respect in a world that constantly told them they were rough, uncultured, animal-like, and a prey to every passing whim and emotion. Primitives condemned all those aspects of popular culture that might provide a warrant for these slurs. A good example of these concerns would be the Loughborough Chartist leader, John Skevington, who had been a Primitive Methodist preacher. At a rally in support of the People's Charter in 1838, he combined attacks on Whigs and Tories with an appeal to his audience to 'Turn away from dog and cock fights', which wasted vitally needed resources, and provided the rulers with a pretext for their contempt of the masses [Richardson in Dews (ed.), 1982, 54; see also Colls, 1977, 99-101]. The practical effects of Primitive Methodist faith were seen above all in a new style of life – orderly, dignified, puritanical, purposive. Within the home, this might mean changes in relationships between spouses, and between parents and children, and the adoption of a new pattern of leisure, centred on the chapel. Valenze, who stresses the appeal of early Primitive Methodism to working-class women, relates this to their concern with strengthening the family unit at a time when it was under heavy strain, and with ensuring collective survival. She quotes a testimony by a Chatham woman, whose home was a 'little hell' until her family were converted by the Bible Christians (a West Country sect, similar to the Primitives), and she comments that 'her confession was actually a story of the transformation of a household' [Valenze, 1982, 166, 97-9]. The effects of Primitive Methodism on working-class communities were more ambiguous. In some respects Methodism was a divisive force. Thompson, for instance, refers to the tendency 'to keep their members apart from the contagion of the unconverted, and to regard themselves as being in a state of civil war with the ale-house and the denizens of Satan's strongholds' [1968, 451-2]. On the other hand, the fact that Methodists so often took on positions as community spokesmen suggests that their qualities were respected even by many of those who did not share their puritan way of life. Moreover, parents who were not themselves chapel-members were soon sending their children to Primitive Methodist Sunday Schools, and themselves sometimes coming along for special events. So the idea of Primitive Methodists as a set-apart sect would only really be applicable to the early years of their establishment in a given area.

But in the middle decades of the nineteenth century Primitive Methodism was changing in character. Kendall [1902, 99], the

29

church's official historian, defined the year 1843 as the beginning of the age of 'consolidation'. About this time a massive programme of chapel-building got under way. New qualities were required of the Primitive preacher: the evangelist was giving way to the pastor and the fund-raiser. The first major casualty was the female travelling preacher, who had been such a prominent part of the heroic age: the last of them went into retirement in 1860, but in fact no new female itinerants had been recruited since 1842. By the 1860s there was a small, but influential, stratum of relatively wealthy Primitives, who were demanding new standards of education and propriety from their preachers. In 1865 the Connexion set up a boarding school for the sons of their élite, and in 1868 there followed the first Primitive Methodist theological college (an idea that would have horrified the movement's founders). Sir William Hartley, a millionaire jam manufacturer, was emerging as a key figure, able to fund developments of which he approved [Turner and Milburn in Dews (ed.), 1982, *8-9, 59-70*].

Nonetheless, the great majority of Primitive Methodists continued to belong to the working class [Field, 1977, *207-9*]. Thus more important than the upward mobility of a small élite were more general changes within the working class during the second half of the nineteenth century.

The third quarter of the nineteenth century was a period when class tensions abated, after the extreme antagonisms of the 1790s to the 1840s, and when working-class voters were integrated into the political system of Liberal/Tory conflict. It was also a period when real wages rose substantially, though the benefits seem to have accrued disproportionately to certain groups of skilled worker. Other important trends included a continuous improvement in the level of literacy, and further rapid urbanisation, so that at the end of the nineteenth century Britain was overwhelmingly a nation of town- and city-dwellers. The most obvious aspect of this was migration from the countryside. But equally significant was the expansion of the great conurbations in south-east Lancashire, west Yorkshire or the west midlands, to swallow up many of the industrial villages which had often been strongholds of Methodism.

Several historians have suggested that the years around the mid-century also mark a turning-point in the history of working-class religion. But there have been two apparently conflicting versions of the change. For Gilbert [1976], working-class involvement in organised religion was highest during the first half of the nineteenth century. He suggests that the great expansion of Nonconformity ground to a halt in the 1840s, and that although the revival of the Church of England began at about the same time, both church and chapel appealed mainly to the middle class in the second half of the nineteenth century. He argues that working-class Nonconformists were heavily concentrated in declining occupations, such as handloom weaving, and that the chapels had little success among the rising number of factory workers and city-dwellers. Furthermore, Gilbert argues that rising prosperity in the later Victorian period was undermining interest in religion in all sections of society by reducing the number of crisis points at which individuals tended to 'turn to' religion, and by encouraging the belief that most human problems could be solved by natural means, and that the world could be continuously and progressively improved [Gilbert, 1976, *112-13, 145-8, 186*-7]. The nub of Gilbert's argument lies in the statistics, which show the members of evangelical Nonconformist denominations as a proportion of the English population expanding rapidly from 1780 to 1840, standing still or slightly declining from 1840 to 1880, and clearly declining thereafter; the explanation offered for this trend is, however, largely hypothetical, and more evidence is needed to substantiate it.

In opposition to Gilbert, we have those, like Wickham [1957, *127, 131-4, 149-50*] who defined the second half of the nineteenth century as the 'years of religious boom' in Sheffield. His main criterion was the building of new churches and chapels. While he too stressed the middle-class character of most congregations, he implied that the working-class element was increasing in this period, whether because of the expansion of Primitive Methodism, or the successful efforts of individual ministers, especially Congregationalists, in attracting working-class congregations [Wickham, 1957, *130*-7]. The mid-Victorian prosperity which, in Gilbert's view, sapped the strength of the churches, was in Wickham's eyes a major factor in the 'religious boom': more resources were available for church-building, many of the new churches being in previously under-provided working-class areas; the church-going lower middle class was rapidly growing in numbers; and there was a 'new habit of chapel-going on the part of superior working-class people' [Wickham, 1957, *127-8, 131*]. Other historians have reached similar conclusions by different routes, notably Foster [1974, *147, 205-15*] who argued that working-class church-going in Oldham increased from the later 1840s onwards from the low levels prevalent in the early decades of the century, the main reason for the increase being declining class-consciousness. This view would seem to be implicitly endorsed by Joyce, who [1980, *178, 317, 337*], in another major interpretation of nineteenth-century Lancashire history, argues that life in the north-western cotton towns was dominated from the 1850s to the 1880s by large, paternalistically run, family firms, in which the bonds between employer and worker were often strengthened by membership of the same churches and chapels; he goes on to suggest that the growth of secularism in the 1880s made an important contribution to undermining employer influence.

The chronologies of religious change offered by these authors can be largely reconciled, though not their proposed explanations. Foster suggests a rise in church-going between the 1820s and the 1850s, with Nonconformist chapels being the main beneficiaries, and this would accord with Gilbert's membership figures, though Foster would see the main increase as coming in the later 1840s, at about the time when Gilbert sees Nonconformist growth as faltering. Wickham's finding that overall church attendance was just keeping pace with population growth between 1851 and 1881 also fits well with Gilbert's figures; both show the Church of England holding its own, with the Congregationalists, and more especially the Wesleyans, losing ground, and the more plebeian branches of Dissent gaining ground. Nonetheless, interpretation of the religious statistics is bedevilled both by the incompleteness of the evidence and by the fact that the figures which are available have not been systematically analysed. Thus we have nationwide church-going figures for 1851, and figures for many towns from 1881, but very little for the earlier part of the century. As far as church membership is concerned, we have excellent Methodist statistics running right through the century; but for other major denominations figures are scarce until the later nineteenth century, and the estimates of Anglican communicants or of Congregationalist members provided by Gilbert should not be taken too literally. As far as the interpretation of these figures is concerned, it seems to me that Gilbert overstates the degree to which the third quarter of the nineteenth century was a period of church decline, and that there is a good deal of sense in Wickham's comments on developments during this period in Sheffield: the fact that the church-going population managed to grow in step with a general city population that doubled in thirty years is strong testimony to the continuing vitality of the churches and chapels; and the fact that the more plebeian denominations, including the Primitive Methodists and the recently established Salvation Army, made up a greater proportion of the church-going population provides some support for Wickham's view that working-class church attendance increased during this period.

While the statistical evidence is unclear, there is no doubt that important qualitative changes in working-class religion took place during the third quarter of the century, and here it is worth returning to the Primitive Methodists.

In the second half of the nineteenth century, Primitives were tending to feel themselves increasingly at home in the world, and their religion was coming to be focused more on a life of service and good citizenship than on the all-out evangelism of earlier years. Bible-reading remained as popular as ever, but Primitives no longer expected that problems of interpretation and application would be settled by dreams and visions. Magic and religion appeared in more open opposition than once had been the case: chapel-goers were believers in progress and enlightenment, and as such had no sympathy with 'superstition'. Neither did they entirely retain the contempt of their forebears for 'worldly' amusements. Certainly, drinking, gambling and sexual promiscuity were taboo, but Nonconformists tended to share the sports mania of their late Victorian contemporaries – the revaluation of 'this' world included a positive view of healthy recreation as a gift of God to be enjoyed. As far as politics were concerned, both the extreme radicalism and the political indifference of earlier years were giving way to a monolithic Liberalism [Obelkevich, 1976, 248-56; Moore, 1974, 159-60; Lawson, 1887, 54, 68-76].

Those Methodists who disliked these trends could join the Salvation Army, which was established in its present form in 1877 and already had about 100,000 members in 1900, though after that growth was much slower [Gilbert, 1976, 42-3]. General and Mrs Booth had been members of the Methodist New Connexion, until they decided to go it alone after their spectacular methods of revivalism ceased to receive the approval of Conference. In some respects the Salvationists were a throwback to early Primitive Methodism: evangelism was their one over-riding concern; they would use any gimmick to gain an audience, and once they had one, they had no qualms about subjecting the unconverted to flame-by-flame descriptions of hell; many of their preachers were women; they were completely apolitical. But in one important respect they fully reflected the development of popular Nonconformity since the early nineteenth century: they accepted, and took to new extremes, the shibboleth of teetotalism.

The British teetotal movement began in 1832. It received some support from secular radicals, but most pioneer teetotallers were Nonconformists from the working and lower middle class; they tended to be supporters of revivalism, and militantly anti-clerical. The issue remained highly divisive in Wesleyan and Primitive Methodism for several decades. Only after about 1860 did teetotalism come to be accepted as a normal part of being a Methodist; by then it had lost most of its more controversial associations [Billington, 1978–9]. The cult of temperance in later Victorian Nonconformity symbolised the transition from a religion of faith to a religion of works. To its later nineteenth-century advocates, temperance meant prosperous and happy homes. It meant new priorities: family outings, better furniture, books. It meant healthy and wholesome sports, like cricket and soccer, rather than games of chance, contests of brute strength, or sports involving animals, in all of which the main interest focused on the associated gambling [cf. Lawson, 1887, 57-66]. The temperance ideal was especially attractive to women: in Dundee the enfranchisement of women was followed by the election of a Prohibitionist MP – who offered the working-class teetotaller the best of both worlds, since on most issues he sided with the Labour Party [Walker, 1979].

Temperance was the supreme embodiment of 'respectability', the word that summed up the ideal of good living held by many working-class Christians of the later nineteenth century. Interviews by Thompson and Vigne with people brought up early this century in strongly church-oriented families give some indications of what this meant in practice. For instance, a man from Oakworth, Yorkshire (born 1903), whose parents worked in a gas works and a textile mill respectively, and who were Congregationalists and socialists, commented that many of those who lived in the mill houses in their village had a low standard of living, because 'the parents went drinking, gambling and all other vices of life. Well my parents didn't do that. Although they were probably same income as a labourer, that made the difference. We'd a home, a respectable working class home, where if you went into these houses they hadn't a home to go into' [Thompson and Vigne, interviews, no. 206, 30]. Church-going families were expected to deny themselves apparently attractive indulgences that could place them on the path to poverty and disgrace. They also generally repudiated anything tainted with charity [Moore, 1974, 142-4]. (While there were some people who went to church in the hope of charity, Thompson and Vigne's interviews suggest that the great majority of working-class church-goers would have been disgusted by the idea.) Similarly, they had a horror of anything dishonest or illegal. Drink often inspired such feelings of revulsion: the taking of the pledge was as much the characteristic moment of the moralistic Christianity of the later nineteenth century, as the experience of conversion had been that of the early nineteenth-century revival period.

On these points, middle-class and working-class church-goers could agree. But the working-class understanding of 'respectability' also included an assertion of their dignity as working-class people, and their entitlement to the same respect as that due to the members of any other class, provided they were morally upright and financially independent. One of the strongest attractions of the churches and chapels for many working-class people lay in the fact that they seemed to offer particularly firm support for an orderly and self-respecting way of life.

This was the culture in which many of the pioneers of the Labour Party grew up. A good example would be Keir Hardie. Born of poor parents in Lanarkshire in 1856, he went down the mine at the age of 10. At 22 he was converted to Christianity and temperance; he joined the Evangelical Union, a mainly working-class church, and became an active member of the Good Templars. Soon after, he became a trade unionist, and acquired a reputation for militancy that led to his being blacklisted. He retained a strong belief in individual self-help and self-discipline. He himself went to night school, and as a miner he studied by day in the darkness at the bottom of the pit. After getting the sack, he was given a job writing a column in a local paper. His advice to his former workmates was to 'drink less, read more and think more'. He was always ready to praise good employers; he was equally ready with moral condemnation of bad employers, and his move to the Left during the 1880s was influenced by the realisation that the latter were increasingly typical in the coal and iron industries. Both his Christianity and his socialism were moralistic and undogmatic [Morgan, 1975, 6-11, 201-10]. All his life he was both an ardent Christian and a severe critic of the churches. An essential part of his moral condemnation of the rich lay in his indignation at the hypocrisy of those who oppressed the poor yet claimed to be devout church-members; he was equally critical of the apparent connivance by the church authorities [Drummond and Bulloch, 1978, 199-201]. Hardie was representative of a good many working-class Christians of the later Victorian period, who adopted a highly practical form of religion that gave a high priority to the achievement of a just and equal society, and who came to believe that labour and socialist organisations were doing more than the churches to bring about the kind of world that they wanted.

# 4  Identity

In eighteenth-century Britain, the Established Churches may have been declining, but they still had a pervasive influence on everyday life. The parish clergy enjoyed considerable prestige, especially in Scotland. Control over parish education, over many parish charities in England, and over the general system of poor relief in Scotland (until 1845) also gave them widespread influence upon the secular affairs of their parishes. The parish church, as the place where the overwhelming majority of the population was baptised, married and buried, was the main symbol of community, even for those who seldom went to church at other times. Indeed, the bitter disputes over patronage (the right to choose the minister) in eighteenth- and nineteenth-century Scotland, and over ritual in nineteenth-century England, reflected the widespread feeling that the parish church belonged to the people, and that it was everyone's concern what went on there [Brown, 1981, *I, 39, 46-8, 57*; McLeod 1974, *187-8*]. In this situation, those who deliberately cut themselves off from the parish church formed a highly visible group, limited to the status of second-class citizens, and regarded with suspicion by their more orthodox neighbours. *The Statistical Account of Scotland* in the 1790s showed that many parish ministers knew the religious affiliation of every family in their parish, and the same was true of many Anglican rural and small town incumbents, who provided their bishops with precise breakdowns of the religious composition of their parishioners. Beliefs were private, but sectarian allegiance was highly public; except in the larger towns or remoter hamlets it was difficult for anyone to remain entirely neutral.

In these circumstances, the great growth of Protestant Dissent from about 1790, and of Roman Catholicism mainly after 1830, had deeply divisive effects. In nineteenth-century Britain, sectarian allegiance was to rank next to class as the most important source of social identity. There were a variety of ways in which this could happen. In a society where theological controversy provoked widespread interest, a wide range of words existed for the purpose of defining those who accepted or rejected particular doctrines (Calvinist and Arminian; baptist and paedobaptist; universalist and conditionalist; atheist, agnostic, deist,

36

theist or pantheist, etc.). These words were seen by many people as reflecting fundamental choices, and the definitions played an important part in the way that they saw themselves and others. But the essential point about nineteenth-century Britain was that society was structured in such a way that sectarian identity influenced most areas of life, and even those least interested in religion found that there were occasions when such an identity was forced upon them.

In areas strongly affected by Irish immigration, notably Lancashire and the west of Scotland, there was by the 1850s (in some places earlier) a fundamental division between Protestant and Catholic. In most other areas, above all in Wales, the main distinction was between church and chapel. Sectarian conflict was in fact endemic in nineteenth-century European societies and it took two main forms. One kind of conflict was an aspect of the decline of the *ancien régime* and the transition to a more democratic and pluralist society; the other was a product of the great mixing of heterogeneous populations following the mass migration of peasants to such thriving industrial zones as Lancashire, northern France and the Ruhr [McLeod, 1981, *15-20, 76-8*]. The antagonism between church and chapel belonged to the first category, that between Protestant and Catholic to the second.

To look first at the division between Catholic and Protestant: for most Irish immigrants Catholicism was an essential part of their national identity and wherever the Irish settled the Catholic parish became a focal point of their community life. When they settled in large numbers, Protestantism tended to become equally self-conscious and aggressive. In parts of Britain with a large Catholic minority, children were brought up throughout the period from the 1850s to the 1930s to be aware of the symbols of their own faith and to regard adherents of the rival religion in terms of a series of hostile stereotypes. In such strongholds of sectarian feeling as Liverpool, Preston or Glasgow, the religious composition of every street came to be common knowledge: in Liverpool, for instance, during the riots of 1909 Protestant and Catholic gangs toured their own parts of the city, evicting neighbours who were of the wrong religion [Waller, 1981, *237-41*].

A century and a half of sectarian brawls in Liverpool had begun on 12 July 1819. There were spasmodic collisions in other towns in the 1830s and 1840s. But it was in the 1850s and 1860s that antagonism between Protestant and Catholic became a basic feature of everyday life in most Lancashire towns and in the Glasgow region. The great increase in the Irish Catholic population in the years following the

Famine gave fresh relevance to evangelical propaganda against Catholic doctrine, and frequently brought immigrant and native into direct competition for jobs. Moreover, Tory politicians soon realised that the exploitation of these economic and religious antagonisms offered a golden opportunity for the rebuilding of their electoral base – especially in view of the collapse of the Chartism that had been so powerful in the 1830s and 1840s [Kirk, in Lunn, 1980; Joyce, 1980, 251-3]. The Tory politicians and the militant evangelicals found energetic allies in the Ulster Protestants who were quite numerous in Liverpool and Glasgow and well-organised in Orange societies, and who helped to ensure that anti-Irish feeling mainly took a sectarian form. Militant Protestantism also offered a formula by which the Anglican clergy were able to appeal beyond the 'respectable' sections of the working class to a wider audience than they attracted elsewhere. Leaders of Toryism and anti-Catholicism in south-east Lancashire in the 1860s included a group of clergy who won a big following by combining a popular and informal style with vocal support for the native worker against Nonconformist employers and Catholic immigrants. In Liverpool, too, Anglican clergy attracted large working-class congregations by arousing, as one of them put it, 'the latent Protestantism of the masses', and by using their churches as centres for Orange activity. Admittedly by the early twentieth century, when sectarian conflict reached its greatest intensity, extreme Protestants were losing faith both in the Church of England (increasingly corrupted by 'ritualism') and in the Conservative Party. In 1903 they set up their own Protestant Reformers church in Liverpool, under the leadership of Pastor George Wise, who claimed the largest congregations in the city, and whose Protestant Party held a place on the City Council for most of the twentieth century [Waller, 1981, 26-7, 207-8, 502].

By the 1850s most British cities had their distinct Irish Catholic neighbourhoods. The effect of attacks by Tory politicians and evangelical preachers, and of violent clashes with native workers, was greatly to reinforce the inner cohesion of these Irish Catholic communities, and to strengthen the sense of Catholic identity among their members. At the time of the religious census in 1851, the lack of churches and priests meant that the level of formal Catholic practice was necessarily fairly low [Lees, 1979, 181-2; McLeod, 1974, 40]. But about this time the church embarked on a big building programme. The task of drawing the immigrant masses into these churches was furthered by a generation of priests, many of them Irish-born, who combined dictatorial methods of leadership in the parish with a determination to attract poor Catholics through colourful Ultra-montane devotions, a wide range of parish organisations, and plenty of free seats [Gilley in Dyos and Wolff (eds), 1973]. During the second half of the nineteenth century the clergy attempted to insulate the faithful from their heretical environment by means of a complete system of separate schools, hospitals, orphanages and charities [Gilley in Lunn (ed.), 1980]. In this instance Ultramontane exclusivism provided a theological rationale for a set-apartness which native hostility largely forced upon the Catholic immigrant. The more moderate forms of Irish nationalism also received strong support from the clergy, though revolutionary Fenianism was generally condemned. Parish organisations appealed most strongly to the 'respectable working class' and lower middle class, many of whom subscribed to an ethos of hard work, saving, temperance and support for the Liberal Party, similar to that espoused by their Nonconformist contemporaries. On the other hand, the poorest Catholics, together with some political activists, alienated by the clergy's opposition to revolutionary violence, and their ambivalent attitude to trade unions, took much less part in parish life, and seldom attended mass. But those who were, in terms of the church's formal requirements 'bad Catholics', usually remained strongly Catholic in loyalty. They championed their churches and priests against any form of Protestant attack, and they were bitterly hostile to those Catholics who betrayed their own people by marrying a Protestant or accepting charity from a Protestant institution [McLeod, 1974, *34-5, 72-80*; Walker, 1979, Chapter 3; Campbell, 1979, *192*].

The division between church and chapel was less clear-out. There is little evidence of residential segregation [though see Joyce, 1980, *176*]; neither does there seem to have been a taboo on intermarriage. Moreover, some people attended church in the morning and chapel in the afternoon, or selected whichever place of worship seemed to offer the most attractive preaching or was most conveniently sited [Pelling, 1968]. Nonetheless, each side had many more committed adherents, and at some times and places the feeling between them could be very bitter. The church/chapel split was far more widespread than the highly localised Protestant/Catholic conflicts, and it was more far-reaching in its effects on nineteenth-century society.

The principal importance of this split lay in the fact that church and chapel symbolised the identity and aspirations of rival élites in their struggle for power, and linked the members of each élite group with a working-class and lower-middle-class following. In the early nine-teenth century, a time of rapid social change and of intense conflict between established élites and the newly rich, the divisions within the middle and upper classes were reflected in membership of different religious denominations. There were no clear-cut doctrinal differences between the Established Churches and the larger Dissenting bodies. (On the whole they did not brand one another as 'heretics' and 'idolators' in the way that poisoned relations between Protestant and Catholic.) But there were major differences on questions of church government; equally important was the fact that the whole ethos of church was quite different from that of chapel. In the circumstances of later eighteenth- and early nineteenth-century Britain, membership of a Dissenting congregation was a criticism not only of the Established Church, but of the whole social-political order of which it was an integral part. For several decades after the 1790s, religious dissent was the most widely attractive means of expressing discontent with the existing order. By the 1830s Dissenters were sufficiently numerous and politically active to form an important electoral bloc in most constituencies, and to dominate many of the reformed municipal corporations. Right up to the time of the First World War, religious issues would be in the forefront of politics.

In the 1830s and 1840s, and again in the 1880s and 1890s, working-class activists tried to sidestep the system of Liberal vs Conservative politics by sponsoring independent Chartist or Labour candidates for Parliament or for local authorities. But before 1906 these efforts met with very limited success. For long periods of time, most activists accepted the necessity of working within the system, and most working-class voters regarded themselves as Liberals or Tories. Sectarian allegiance exercised a crucial influence on which identity they chose.

Two factors that helped to maintain a high level of sectarian consciousness in the working class were the hiring practices of the small and medium-sized family firms, and the patterns of educational provision before the direct intervention of the state in the 1870s.

The pioneers in the great expansion of basic education from the late eighteenth century onwards were the Sunday Schools. While many were started by private individuals or by interdenominational com-mittees, the latter soon fell apart under the weight of sectarian rivalry and political tensions. Radical, Chartist (and later, Socialist) Sunday Schools were also established at many points, but they remained very small by comparison with their church- and chapel-based counterparts.

By 1851 the overwhelming majority of Sunday scholars were enrolled in denominational schools, and a very high proportion of working-class children were spending at least some time in them [Laqueur, 1976, *45*; Evans, 1977, *332-49*; Brown, 1981, II, *20*]. For much of the nineteenth century, attendance at Sunday Schools was substantially higher than at day schools; but weekday elementary education also tended to be sponsored by churches or by societies with strong sectarian associations. In England and Wales the major bodies were the predominantly Nonconformist British Society (founded 1807) and the Anglican National Society (founded 1811). In Scotland, privately-run schools had a bigger role, but interdenominational competition was a major stimulus to the expansion of schooling. The formation of school boards in 1870 led to a gradual decline in the number of denominational schools; but in some areas, notably Lancashire, they remained dominant well into the twentieth century; in Scotland, the various Presbyterian denominations ceased to run separate schools – one step towards the formation of a reunited Church of Scotland in 1929 – but the distinction remained between the non-sectarian, but essentially Protestant, board schools and the Roman Catholic schools, which remained outside the system.

The value of schools as agencies of indoctrination can easily be exaggerated. Then, as now, many children were reluctant scholars, who left as soon as they could, having absorbed as little as possible of what the school was attempting to teach. Nonetheless, there is quite a lot of evidence that Sunday Schools were fairly widely popular, partly because of the skill with which they mixed religion and education with entertainments and outings, and that they evoked strong loyalties from at least some of their students [Laqueur, 1976, *169-79*; Roberts, 1976, *86-7*; Evans, 1977, *332-49*; Joyce, 1980, *247-8*]. And while much of the education provided was uncontentious in nature, and differed little from one school to another, tribal loyalties were nourished by the annual Whit Walks, and by the practice of bringing the children on to the streets to demonstrate for and against legislation that affected the interests of their church. Roman Catholic day schools were particularly explicit in their attempts to develop a strong sense of sectarian identity [Joyce, 1980, *245-50*; Elizabeth Roberts, interviews with Mrs P1P, *2*, and Mr F1P, *9*].

While the schools helped children to grow up with the sense of being Anglicans, Methodists, and so on, the hiring practices of many firms ensured that these loyalties were not forgotten in adulthood. Employers tried to forge links with their workforce by giving preference to members of their own denomination. In Liverpool and in the Lanarkshire mining district, some employers had links with the Orange Order, while others were equally strongly Catholic. In many northern textile towns there were Anglican mills and Nonconformist mills. Some small employers would give a job to anyone who attended the same place of worship as themselves [Shallice, 1979–80, *21-2*; Campbell, 1979, *223-4*; E. T. Davies, 1965, *149-51*; Joyce, 1980, *172-7*]. Others built a church or chapel for the benefit of their employees and then more or less compelled them to attend it.

Where sectarian animosities were fiercest, trade union organisation was often weak [Campbell, 1979, *194, 237*]. One reason was that in such situations every working-class organisation took on some kind of denominational colouring and failed to attract members of other churches. The most dramatic example was the great quarry strike at Bethesda in Caernarvonshire in 1900–3, which was strongly supported by the Calvinistic Methodist chapels. On the other hand, Anglican workers tended to identify more closely with their Tory Anglican employer, Lord Penrhyn, than with their Nonconformist colleagues, and most of them went on working. Moreover, as starving strikers drifted back to work, they left their chapels, where they were regarded as traitors, and started going to the church [R. M. Jones, 1981]. Sectarian consciousness tended to be strongest in areas such as north Wales, Liverpool or the Scottish Highlands (with its English-speaking lairds and Gaelic-speaking Free Kirk crofters), where religious differences were linked to differences of language or nationality. But even without such reinforcement, opposing symbols and ideals, and often important differences in life-style, divided the adherents of rival sects. Dissenters generally saw their chapels as bastions of freedom, democracy and equality of opportunity, and were inclined to regard churchpeople as snobs or sycophants. Churchpeople prided themselves on broader minds and wider culture, claimed a special affinity with the Royal Family, saw themselves as the truest British patriots, and dismissed Dissenters as puritanical bigots. The mutual stereotyping is well conveyed in a journalistic account of Blackburn in 1867: '. . . it is a thorough-going Tory community. Strong drink is the secret of its own and Britain's greatness; after that its heart has been given for long years to the Church and cockfighting. Be sober, lead a decent and respectable life and your genuine Blackburner will wax red at the mention of your name, and dismiss you as "a –Dissenter"' [Joyce, 1980, *187*].

Thompson and Vigne's interviews with men and women born

between 1872 and 1906 show how sharply sectarian divisions were reflected in voting habits. Among 72 respondents brought up in working-class families in the industrial districts of north-eastern England, Yorkshire, the north midlands and south Wales, 16 per cent of those with a chapel-going father stated that he voted Tory during the period before the First World War, as against 38 per cent of those whose father went nowhere, and 67 per cent of those with church-going Anglican fathers. More surprisingly, if non-church-going fathers are assigned to the denomination of the Sunday School attended by their children, there is little difference between the voting habits of the church-going and non-church-going members of the denomination. Thus 64 per cent of non-church-going fathers with children at Anglican schools voted Tory, but only 25 per cent of those with children at Nonconformist schools. This suggests that the choice of school was less random than Pelling [1968, 30], for example, suggests, and that it reflected a sense of sectarian identity that most people felt, in however tenuous a degree.

# 5  Working-Class Politics

These working-class Anglicans and Nonconformists at the end of the nineteenth century were following a lead that had been emphatically provided by their ministers. Throughout the nineteenth century, the clergy of the major British denominations were deeply involved in the party political system. Surviving English poll-books from the years 1830–72 show that the Anglican clergy voted more heavily for Tory candidates than did those in any secular occupation. Conversely, Nonconformist ministers and Roman Catholic priests voted overwhelmingly for Whig, Liberal or Radical candidates. In Wales, the church–Tory and chapel–Liberal links were equally strong, and perhaps even more significant, because the part played by the churches in Welsh life was greater than it was in England. In Scotland, prior to the Disruption of 1843, Whigs and Tories had allied with rival factions in the Established Church; thereafter the denominational pattern soon became as clear as it was south of the border. By the 1870s ministers of the Old Kirk were heavily Tory, while those of the Free Kirk and United Presbyterians were almost unanimously Liberal [Pelling, 1967, 374]. These patterns of alliances had deep roots, and the only other major change in the first half of the nineteenth century had been the decline of the Toryism that John Wesley had bequeathed to the Wesleyan branch of Methodism, and which remained strong among the generation of preachers who had reacted very negatively to the French Revolution and rallied to the defence of the threatened 'Constitution' in successive crises from 1795 onwards [see Stigant, 1971].

Given the strength of these alliances, independent working-class political organisations seldom received much support from ministers of the larger denominations. Even those who were otherwise sympathetic to working-class demands remained emotionally bound to Liberalism or Toryism. Thus in the 1830s, Anglican clergy who took a lead in campaigning for factory reform or against the New Poor Law were, like Parson Bull of Bierley, 'Tory Radicals' rather than Chartists. A Nonconformist democrat, like the Reverend Edward Miall, who as Disestablishment candidate for Parliament in 1845 supported all six points of the People's Charter, gave priority to religious issues. Few followed the example of the Reverend Patrick Brewster, minister of the Church of Scotland's Paisley Abbey church, who became a prominent Chartist [cf. Faulkner, 1916].

In the later nineteenth century these alliances were being slowly eroded. On the Nonconformist side, the split in the Liberal Party in 1886 saw a fair number of ministers (as well as many wealthy laymen) joining Joseph Chamberlain in Liberal Unionism, and ultimately the drift towards Toryism. At the other end of the political spectrum, the formation of the Independent Labour Party in 1893 was followed by a steady trickle of Nonconformist ministers into the socialist camp. Nonetheless, on the eve of the First World War, Nonconformist ministers generally remained vocal supporters of the Liberal Party, hopeful that working-class interests could be adequately served by a radical Liberal government, combining a progressive welfare policy with concern for old Nonconformist issues, such as non-sectarian education and temperance.

On the Established Church side, Toryism remained predominant at the turn of the century, but from the 1870s onwards some clergy in working-class parishes were showing an interest in Christian Socialism. In the Church of England the pioneer was Stewart Headlam who, as a curate in the East End of London in 1877, founded the Guild of St Matthew, which combined advocacy of land nationalisation with attacks on the puritanism of many clergy. Ironically, its members mainly came from the traditionally conservative High Church: many High Anglican clergy had been turned into rebels by their experience of persecution by Low Church bishops and by Disraeli's Conservative government, and some were beginning to realise that their corporate understanding of the church could easily be converted into a corporate understanding of society, sharply critical of the prevailing competitive individualism [P. Jones, 1968]. In Scotland a Christian Socialist movement developed among the clergy of cities like Glasgow at about the same time. While most of them preferred single-issue crusades to membership of a working-class party, one of the founders of the Glasgow ILP (Independent Labour Party), John Glasse, was a Church of Scotland minister [Brown, 1981, I, 516].

Though the clergy tended to determine the official stance of their churches, they did not necessarily speak for the lay membership. In nineteenth-century Britain, as at most other points in church history, there were frequently tensions between clergy and laity, between higher and lower clergy, or between lay leaders and rank and file. It should not be assumed that the 'political effects' of Methodism,

Roman Catholicism, and so on can be determined by studying statements made by the church's leaders. Nonetheless, it is true that church leaders could make things very uncomfortable for those who took a political line different from their own, especially in the more centralised denominations, such as the Roman Catholic Church, and the various branches of Methodism and of Scottish Presbyterianism. There were thus heavy concentrations of radicals in certain small and somewhat eccentric, or even openly heterodox, religious bodies. The most theologically conventional examples were the Independent Methodists, who started in Warrington in 1796, set up many new branches in Lancashire and the north-east in the 1820s, when radical Methodists were being expelled from the Wesleyan Connexion, and had close links with Chartism in some areas in the 1840s and 1850s [Ward, 1972, *92-3*; Valenze, 1982, *223-56*]. It is significant that Independent Methodists differed from other branches of the movement in that each church was autonomous and that their ministers were unpaid. (They also, like the early Primitive Methodists, made no distinction between the roles of women and of men [Ward, 1972, *93*; Wilkinson in Davies, George and Rupp (eds), 1978, *325*].) Consequently, the Independents were spared the development of a class of paid preachers with perspectives and priorities different from those of most lay members, as happened in early nineteenth-century Wesleyanism [cf. Ward, 1972, Chapter 4], and there was no all-powerful Conference to whip the *avant-garde* into line, as there was, not only in the Wesleyan Connexion, but among the New Connexion and the Primitives too. Congregational autonomy also meant that it was possible for individual Baptist and Congregational churches to go far beyond the cautious reformism prevalent in the denomination as a whole. But political radicalism frequently grew out of religious heterodoxy. In the early nineteenth century the Unitarians were a notable example, combining as they did congregational autonomy with doctrines that made them pariahs in the eyes of many of their neighbours. Besides the prestigious city-centre chapels, which were to become strongholds of upper-middle-class Liberalism, there were, at least in Lancashire, a number of working-class chapels. In Oldham two Unitarian chapels appear to have had a major role in the early development of working-class radicalism from the 1790s to the 1810s [Foster, 1974, *35-8, 279-80*]. The same link between heterodoxy and radicalism is illustrated by the example of two small, but locally important, bodies formed by preachers expelled from the Wesleyans and the Methodist New Connexion for heretical doctrine: the Cookites

46

or Methodist Unitarians, who originated in Rochdale in 1806, and the Barkerites, who flourished in the West Riding and the north-east in the 1840s. Both groups were strongly involved in Chartism; though the Methodist Unitarians' chief claim to fame is the fact that at least half the Rochdale Pioneers of Co-operation belonged to their church [Wilkinson in Davies, George and Rupp (eds), 1978]. Other relatively small and obscure religious groups who seem to have had an important role in the development of working-class radicalism within certain localities were the Swedenborgians, who were quite strong in Manchester and Salford in the first half of the nineteenth century, and the Spiritualists, who established themselves in England in 1852, and whose major centre was Keighley [Lineham and Barrow in Shiels (ed.), 1982, *212-14, 232*].

However, the most important example of the political implications of religious heterodoxy was the role of secularism in working-class radical movements from the 1790s onwards [see Royle, 1974, 1980; Budd, 1977]. In the early 1820s a militant anti-Christian, Richard Carlile, briefly emerged as the outstanding leader of working-class radicalism, as a result of his untiring campaign for freedom of the press, meaning in practice freedom to publish anti-Christian or radical books and newspapers. His publication of Paine's *Age of Reason* led to his imprisonment for blasphemy. That in turn led to a nationwide revival of interest in Paine's notorious book, and the formation of a network of clubs for the support of Carlile and the propagation of his views. For the next hundred years every working-class radical movement had a secularist element of varying degrees of size and importance with it. The anti-Christian component was particularly important in the Owenite movement of the 1830s and 1840s. When the movement collapsed, Owenites moved *en masse* into the Secular Societies formed in the 1850s. These flourished under the charismatic leadership of Charles Bradlaugh in the 1860s and 1870s, when they gathered considerable support from politically active skilled workers, especially in Lancashire and Yorkshire. Secularism (meaning opposition to all churches, rather than any specific theological position) provided a unifying principle for radical Liberals involved in a wide range of other campaigns, including republicanism and advocacy of birth control. Organised secularism reached a peak in the 1880s, mainly because of the interest aroused by Bradlaugh's campaign to take his seat in Parliament: thereafter it rapidly declined. Many secularists moved into the newly-formed Social Democratic Federation through which route the old 'infidel' tradition was carried on into the modern

Labour and Communist Parties, though it no longer had the central role which it had enjoyed in many nineteenth-century radical agitations. Secularists were less likely to have the emotional ties with people of more conventional political persuasions which complicated the loyalties of the radical who was also a church-member. They had an important part among the pioneers of new directions in working-class politics, and among the hard core who remained active through thick and thin.

But, in spite of the continuing importance of deists and atheists among the leaders of working-class radical movements, the appeal of secularism was never very wide. The characteristic religious product of such periods of high political excitement as 1838–42 and the early 1890s was not any increase in support for secularism, but the formation of Chartist and Labour Churches. The Chartist Churches began in the Glasgow area; they later spread south of the border, but without achieving the same degree of popularity. Their leaders were mostly people who had been active Dissenters, but had become frustrated by the extremely cautious, and sometimes hostile, attitude of their ministers to the new movement. At the height of Scottish Chartism from 1839 to 1842, weekly religious services, with Bible-reading, psalm-singing and sermons, were being organised by the Chartists in most Scottish towns, even where no church had been formally organised; in the movement's declining years, the surviving Chartist Churches seem to have been the main centres of continuing activity. According to Wilson [1970] it was an essential part of the case made by the Scottish Chartists that they were the authentic practitioners of the principles of social justice proclaimed by the Old Testament prophets, and of the equality of all mankind taught in the New Testament. The Labour Church movement began by a reverse process, the founder, John Trevor, being a Manchester Unitarian minister who had become frustrated by the conservatism of his wealthy congregation. He decided that a new kind of church was needed which would attract working-class people, and he accordingly organised the first Labour Church service, with 400 people present, in Manchester in 1891. In 1892 and 1893 Labour Churches were formed all over industrial Britain, the densest concentration being round Manchester. Sometimes the circumstances were dramatic. During the 1892 election in Bradford, F. W. Jowett, leader of a group of Nonconformist socialists, was prevented from speaking at a rally of Nonconformists in support of the Liberal candidate: he retaliated by announcing that he and his friends would found a Labour Church.

The Labour Church experiment proved short-lived in most places. As meeting places which could be shared by the diverse elements in the Labour and socialist movement, and which could, in the phraseology of the time, provide a 'Sunday home' for these who felt out of place in the other churches, they served an important function. But there was no consensus, once the first flush of enthusiasm had died down, as to what the religious basis of the movement should be. The movement foundered because there were so many theologically incompatible elements within the socialist movement (ranging from orthodox Nonconformists, via Unitarians and William Morris socialists, to Marxists), who were initially attracted by the Labour Church idea, but soon found that they could only work together by keeping religious issues in the background. At least 121 Labour Churches were founded in Britain between 1891 and the First World War, but only 13 survived in 1914, and by the 1930s only the Stockport and Hyde branches were left [Summers, 1958, *2-15, 311-17, 367-9, 678-90*].

Thus, in the long run, it was a choice between the 'orthodox' churches or none at all. And in the late nineteenth and early twentieth centuries these churches, especially the Methodists and Roman Catholics, still had a substantial membership in many of the major industrial regions. Some of the most controversial questions in the religious history of the nineteenth and early twentieth centuries concern the relationship between these churches and the labour movement. One tradition of historical interpretation has seen the strength of various forms of Christianity, most notably Methodism, as a major obstacle to the development of working-class radicalism in the period from the 1790s to the 1840s; other historians have stressed the 'Methodist contribution' to working-class political consciousness and organisation. Conversely, the fact that the beginnings of the modern labour movement in the 1880s and 1890s coincides with the beginnings of declining church membership has led some historians to suggest that the latter facilitated the former; while others have stressed the Christian character of much of the British socialism of the period from the 1880s to the 1920s.

The bitterest controversy has surrounded the period from the 1790s to the 1840s. This was a time when both evangelicalism and radicalism gained wide support in the working class. It was also a time when working-class political activity was severely repressed at various points, when a vast amount of peaceful agitation received little tangible reward, and when the few attempts at armed uprisings were a complete failure. The connections between the popularity of evangelicalism, especially Methodism, and these various other facets of the political history of the time have been argued more or less continuously from that day to this. Conservative Methodists argued at the time, in their attempt to secure official favours, that only Methodism 'saved England from revolution' [Ward, 1972, *62, 89-90*]. A bewildering variety of views have been advanced by present-day historians, both in support of such claims and in opposition to them.

Among those historians who have stressed the reactionary role of Methodism, by far the most influential and the most controversial has been E. P. Thompson [1968]. He suggests that the years after Wesley's death in 1791 saw: 'the consolidation of a new bureaucracy of ministers who regarded it as their duty to manipulate the submissiveness of their followers and to discipline all deviant growths within the Church which could give offence to authority. In this they were very successful' *[386]*. Constant subjection to conservative political indoctrination 'could reduce the Methodist working man to one of the most abject of human beings'; in support of this claim, he quotes contemporary accusations that Methodists had acted as spies for government or employers *[429-30]*. If some Methodists were radicals, this was a reaction against the authoritarianism of their leaders, rather than any expression of authentic Methodism *[433]*. A second view, advanced many years ago by Wearmouth [1937], and recently updated by Gilbert [1978-9], presents Methodism, and other popular evangelical movements, as forces for moderate reform which helped to produce an independent-minded and politically-active working class, but militated against violence or illegality.

Thompson, in fact, accepts that there was general participation by Methodists in Chartism in some areas [1968, *433*], so that his difference with Gilbert seems to be largely a matter of chronology and interpretation. Gilbert sees Methodism, and similar evangelical movements, as containing an implicit element of social protest from the start, and as contributing to the mental emancipation of the working class, whereas Thompson, whose position is less explicit, appears to see Methodists being drawn, in spite of themselves, into movements that had already become very strong in their localities.

Gilbert's and Thompson's work on Methodism must be regarded as brilliant attempts to co-ordinate a wide range of evidence, in order to present a coherent picture of the relationship between popular religion and politics on a national scale. But the validity of their arguments can only effectively be tested by much more detailed research in particular localities. However, there are some reasons for scepticism about both attempts to assign a consistent political role to Methodism. For instance, Gilbert's presentation of Methodists (and also Baptists and Independents) as a force for moderate and peaceful reform might be applicable to the second half of the nineteenth century, but in the early years of the century they do not seem to have limited themselves to peaceful or law-abiding forms of protest. For instance, in January 1813, when fourteen Luddites were hanged at York, they walked to the scaffold singing a Methodist hymn, and it was said that they were all Methodists – much to the disgust of Jabez Bunting, then superintendent of the Halifax circuit, who refused to conduct the funeral of one of them [E. P. Thompson, 1968, *639-41*]. There was further fury from the Wesleyan élite when it was discovered that Isaac Ludlam, hanged for his part in the rising at Pentridge in Derbyshire in 1817, was a local preacher [E. P. Thompson, 1968, *433, 732*]. While Thompson's account of the objectives and methods of the Wesleyan leadership is convincing, he provides very little evidence of their efforts succeeding. On the other hand, there is very extensive evidence (much of which Thompson himself mentions) that they often failed. The numerous secessions and expulsions from Wesleyan Methodism, from the New Connexion in the 1790s to the Wesleyan Reformers at the end of the 1840s, are one measure of this failure. But there also are some hints that the majority who remained had not been effectively indoctrinated with Toryism or quietism. For instance, at Newcastle in 1819 a Wesleyan local preacher, William Stephenson, spoke at a rally held to protest against the Peterloo massacre. The superintendent of Stephenson's North Shields circuit was furious. But a leaders' meeting decided not to strike him off the plan, as three-quarters of Methodists in the circuit were thought to be radical reformers, and they feared the possible repercussions [Stigant, 1971, *111-13*].

It is clear that two quite different versions of Methodism were in collision [cf. Ward, 1972, *85-6*]; there is no reason why we should take the preachers' definition as normative, and that of the radical Methodists as aberrant. Eileen Yeo's analysis [1981, *109*] of the role of religion in the Chartist period seems relevant here: Christianity, she argued, was not 'the possession of any one social group' but 'contested territory', which Whigs, Tories and Chartists all tried to claim as their own. The Bible provided a common language shared by radicals and reactionaries, which both used to press their own claims. Yeo's argument would be consistent with the more sceptical assessment of the political effects of Methodism offered by Hobsbawm [1964, *23-33*], who suggests that Methodists differed little in their politics from others in the same localities and occupations. The spread of Methodism was an aspect of the growing working-class self-consciousness and activism during this period, without being an independent influence on it. Rather similar conclusions were reached in a lively review of early nineteenth-century Wesleyan history by Kent [in Davies, George and Rupp (eds), 1978, *259-69*]. Both regard the claims made for Methodism, by friends and by foes, as exaggerated: other factors besides the possible influence of Methodism are sufficient to explain the effectiveness of factory-work-discipline and the containment of working-class political activity. In any case, if the conditions had otherwise been favourable for a working-class uprising, the Methodists would have been too few to prevent it happening. The last point is questionable: as Gilbert points out, there were heavy concentrations of Methodists, and of other Nonconformists, in many of the industrial areas, and in the social groups most prone to radicalism; also, the number of people attending Methodist and other Nonconformist services during this period far exceeded the number of members, so that membership statistics are not necessarily an adequate index of the extent of evangelical influence. However, the other points made by Hobsbawm and Kent seem convincing.

With the decline of Chartism in the later 1840s and 1850s, it becomes much more possible to see churches and chapels as politically cohesive forces. From the 1850s to the 1880s, the correlation between religious and political affiliation was probably stronger than at any other time. Joyce [1980] relates the inner cohesion of church and chapel in the factory districts of Lancashire to the power of industrial paternalism. Having stressed the influence of employers on the building and running of places of worship, he concludes that 'organised religion was a principal support of employer hegemony' and that it was 'one of the many elements nurturing the sense of commitment to the employer and his territory' [*178*]. It did this both by forming personal ties between employer and worker, and by laying the basis for the sectarian, party and ethnic conflict which provided a focus for the frustrations of the workers and, for most of the time, diverted them from criticism of their own employers and of the industrial system.

Joyce's arguments gain some support from studies of the mining districts of south Wales and Co. Durham at a slightly later date – c.1870–1900. In these areas religious life was dominated by Nonconformity, politics by Liberalism. Many of the coalowners and managers were Nonconformists, and the same was true of the two outstanding union leaders, William Abraham and John Wilson. Shared religious and political convictions seem to have made for harmonious relations. Miners' leaders like Wilson and Abraham argued for the essential compatibility between the interests of workers and owners, and for the possibility of resolving all disputes by negotiation; similarly, the owners made no attempt to crush the unions [Moore, 1974; Morgan, 1981]. Moore supplements the familiar regional picture by detailed study of a group of collieries in the Deerness Valley of Co. Durham. Esh Winning and Waterhouses, with paternalist Quaker owners and conciliatory Primitive Methodist union leaders, was a microcosm of the situation prevailing in the later nineteenth century. When industrial relations on the coalfield deteriorated in the early twentieth century, these collieries held on to their non-militant record.

Nonetheless, Joyce probably overstates the degree to which religious life in the centres of industrial paternalism was taken over by the employers and drained of its potential for social criticism. In the first place, shared religion was not in itself sufficient to ensure harmony between owners and union leaders: owners and managers also had to behave in a way deemed consistent with their religion. Cornsay colliery, a few miles from Esh Winning, had a Methodist manager who was generally regarded as a tyrant; the colliery had a record of militancy, and became a centre of Methodist radicalism [Moore, 1974, 85, 165, 169-82]. A second point is that besides the large employer-patronised churches and chapels which dominated the major thoroughfares of many industrial towns, there were also many less pretentious places of worship, often hidden in back streets, with a more plebeian leadership [Phillips, 1982, 15, 46-51; Cox, 1982, 136-42]. And in factory villages, where everyone lived in the shadow of the mill, any public building which was not provided by an employer stood out as a symbol of independence. For instance, in Oakworth, Yorkshire, at the beginning of this century, the Wesleyans were closely linked with one big mill, and the Anglicans with the other, but the Congregational chapel, according to one of its members, was a 'congregational Free Speech place' and 'a working man's institution' [Thompson and Vigne interviews, no. 206, 28; see also Drummond and Bulloch, 1978, 164-5]. Furthermore, those who did remain in high-status congregations or clergy-dominated denominations did not necessarily passively follow the lead provided by priests or denominational élite.

When socialism began to catch on in the 1880s and 1890s, and more

53

especially in the early twentieth century, it often took a Christian form. Hobsbawm [1971, *140-1*] noted how many of the trade union and socialist leaders of this period came from a background of teenage conversion and lay preaching. Moore's account of the Deerness Valley provides striking examples from an area admittedly somewhat remote and unusually dominated by Methodism. Most of the pioneers of the ILP in that area were Primitive Methodists, and they worked out a form of socialism that was based on the Bible, though they also drew on a wide range of other sources, from F. D. Maurice and Tolstoy, to Edward Carpenter and Robert Blatchford [Moore, 1974, Chapter 7]. Similarly, Ainsworth [1977] suggests that socialism as it developed in east Lancashire in the later nineteenth century was strongly influenced by the Nonconformist traditions of the area, and that socialists tended to stress the Christian basis of their socialism, even when they dropped their formal church ties. On the other hand, E. P. Thompson has attempted to deflate claims that Nonconformity had a major influence on the formation of the ILP in Yorkshire. While admitting the heavy use of biblical rhetoric in ILP propaganda, he highlights the opposition presented by the 'Nonconformist "Establishment"', and argues that the ILP was 'as much a revolt *against* organised Christianity as a form of Christian expression' ['Homage to Tom Maguire,' in A. Briggs and J. Saville (eds) *Essays in Labour History* (1960)].

Perhaps the most important point made by Thompson with regard to the religious background of the ILP is how varied this background was. The Yorkshire pioneers included several Nonconformists, a Roman Catholic, two Secularists, a disciple of Edward Carpenter, and others with no known religious or anti-religious affiliation. The ILP and later the Labour Party, were essentially non-sectarian (although, by the 1930s, the Roman Catholic element in the Labour Party would be very strong in some areas). Nonetheless, it does seem that in the late nineteenth and early twentieth centuries socialism exercised a particularly strong attraction for young Nonconformists, and the spread of socialism often had very divisive effects within Nonconformist communities. The early twentieth century was a particularly traumatic period for Welsh Nonconformity. The numerous chapels of the mining valleys had a large working-class membership, and a middle-class lay leadership that was strongly tied to the Liberal Party. Some socialist activists were forced out of their chapels in a manner reminiscent of the Buntingite persecutions of radical Methodists in the 1820s. Among the victims was A. J. Cook, whose first fame had been as a Baptist boy preacher, and who was to be secretary of the miners' union at the time of the general strike. Others, like Arthur Horner, another former lay preacher and future miners' leader, lost faith in Christianity and found a comprehensive alternative in 'scientific' socialism. Even so, the completeness of the break can be exaggerated: by the 1920s, many of the chapel-goers in Mardy, the 'Little Moscow' of the Rhondda Valleys, were active in the Labour Party, and a few in the Communist Party [S. Macintyre, *Little Moscows*, 1980; cf. E. T. Davies, 1965, *166-8*; Morgan, 1981, *193-9*].

Horner himself confirms a point made by Ainsworth: that there were close parallels between the appeal of Christianity and of socialism. He wrote that his period as a Baptist boy preacher was a 'definite stage in my political development':

I was desperately conscious of the poverty, the oppression and the injustice around me. I saw in religion the hope and the opportunity to do something about it and in the chapels I had a ready-made audience. I believed in Christianity, but to me it was an empty thing unless linked with practical measures to relieve all these social evils. So my sermons gradually became more and more political in content and soon I began to arouse opposition in the chapels and among some of the deacons where they did not want their religion mixed with politics. For a long time I was trying in my own mind to wed Christianity to Socialism and only slowly did I reach the point of accepting the materialistic conception of history and the struggle of the working class as the only way to emancipation. [A. Horner, *Incorrigible Rebel*, 1960, p. 14]

There are several points here that would apply to many others of the pioneers of British socialism in the late nineteenth and early twentieth centuries. Horner's Christianity and his socialism were motivated by very similar forces of idealism and humanitarian concern, and for a long time the two were closely related in his life. Horner's conversion to socialism did not at first seem to conflict with his religious convictions but to be a natural expression of them. The fact that the two did eventually come into serious conflict, so that his socialism superseded his Christianity, had several causes. One was the opposition that he faced from more conservative chapel authorities. This was an experience shared by many of the Christian socialists of this period, but it need not in itself have been sufficient to cause the break. For instance, the Catholic Socialist Society, formed in 1906 by John Wheatley, later a Glasgow MP and the first Labour Health Minister, faced constant opposition from the Roman Catholic authorities but Wheatley never wavered in his determination to be both a Catholic and a socialist, and to demonstrate that the two were compatible [see Gilley, in Lunn (ed.). 1980]. There were two other factors which were important in making possible the alienation of Horner, and many like him, from their Christian origins: the availability and attractions of Marxism as a complete alternative view of life, and the development in the first quarter of the twentieth century of a socialist subculture, which provided its adherents with a spiritual home, as fully as the churches did for theirs. In Horner's own case, the first factor seems to have been the more important: for the relatively few convinced Marxists, historical materialism tended to preclude Christian faith. But the second factor is of wider significance in explaining the fact that the socialists of this period were often both Christian and largely independent of church influences. The tendency for socialists to form a complete alternative society never reached anything like the proportions in Britain that it did in, for instance, Germany or Austria between the 1890s and the 1930s [cf. McLeod, 1981, 45-7]; nor was there an alienation of socialists from the churches on a scale in any way comparable with what happened in those countries. However, especially in south Wales and the west of Scotland and to a lesser extent in most other industrial districts, the same tendencies could be seen in Britain. The Labour Churches were a first step in this direction, though in most areas they proved a temporary phase. Clarion Clubs, Socialist Sunday Schools, the Women's Co-op Guild, all served to build up the sense of common belonging, and to isolate socialists from hostile influences. Political work brought believers and unbelievers, and members of different denominations, together in pursuit of common socialist objectives. In practice, socialism tended to become a complete way of life, which largely superseded the churches in their social role, without directly challenging the Christian faith.

# 6 Towards Indifference

Perhaps the most famous comment on nineteenth-century working-class religion was that made by Horace Mann in his report on the religious census of 1851 in England and Wales [clviii]. Noting that 'a sadly formidable proportion of the English people are habitual neglecters of the public ordinances of religion', he took it as obvious that most of the absentees were drawn from the working class. After stating that 'in cities and large towns, it is observable how absolutely insignificant a portion of the congregations is composed of artisans', he went on to discuss the reasons for this conspicuous absence from public worship:

> There is a sect, originated recently, adherents to a system called 'Secularism' .... This is the creed which probably with most exactness indicates the faith which, virtually, though not professedly, is entertained by the masses of our working population; by the skilled and unskilled labourer alike – by hosts of minor shopkeepers and Sunday traders – and by miserable denizens of courts and crowded alleys. They are *unconscious Secularists* – engrossed by the demands, the trials, or the pleasures of the passing hour, and ignorant or careless of the future. These are never, or but seldom seen in our religious congregations; and the melancholy fact is thus impressed upon our notice that the classes which are most in need of the restraints and consolations of religion are the classes which are most without them.

Mann was the most eloquent exponent of a view that was heard frequently in nineteenth-century England and Scotland, though less often in Wales. As we have seen, this assessment over-simplified a very complex situation. Yet it clearly pinpointed one very important dimension: the fact that a large part of the working class played little or no part in organised religious life.

There was nothing new about working-class non-church-going. But in the 1830s and 1840s acute social crisis, instilling the whole of the middle and upper classes with a fear of revolution, coincided with a time of renewed evangelistic concern on the part of the clergy of the

57

Established Churches, and these considerations combined to give fresh urgency to a very old problem. Certainly Anglican Visitation Returns throughout the eighteenth century record plenty of complaints from clergy that the poor were largely missing from their congregations [Gilbert, 1976, 10-12]. The Church of Scotland was historically very weak in the Highlands, and in spite of numerous religious revivals in the first half of the nineteenth century, church attendance in 1851 was still lower in Argyllshire and Invernessshire than in any major city. Those immigrants to the cities and industrial villages who seldom went to church were often simply continuing customs that were well established in the countryside. Both in town and countryside members of the upper and middle classes were under much heavier social pressure than the poor to attend some kind of church; even those with little interest in religion had reasons for church-going that did not apply to their working-class counterparts. There also were good reasons why the poor were likely to be less interested in the services of the Established Churches or of many of the Dissenting denominations. The Reformation was a victory for the religion of the word, over the religion of ritual and symbol – for the literate minority, at the expense of the illiterate masses. In some areas, including north-western England and north Wales, the reformers were much more successful in suppressing Catholicism than in establishing Protestantism [cf. Haigh in *Past & Present*, no. 93, 1981]. In such areas something of a religious vacuum developed, which was only effectively filled by the popular evangelical movements of the later eighteenth and early nineteenth centuries. More generally, the post-Reformation church seems to have lost much of the aura that surrounded the medieval church. Magic continued to play an essential part in the lives of the rural population, but gradually it came to be largely dissociated from the church [Obelkevich, 1976, Chapter 6]. There was also the question of whether the poor could ever be fully integrated into congregations where the whole tone was so clearly set by their social 'superiors', where hierarchical seating arrangements emphasised their inferiority, where sermons and prayers spoke the language of the élite and echoed their concerns, where the minister was himself a member of the élite, and on intimate terms with landlords and employers. The poor who did attend such churches were likely to feel themselves marginal members of the congregation.

Developments in the first half of the nineteenth century emphasised this sense of marginality, and led to further alienation of the poor from the Established Churches and also from many Dissenting congregations. This was a formative period in the development of the identity and values both of the working class and of the middle class. The middle class were busily distancing themselves from everything that seemed rough, uncultured and vulgar. At the same time, members of the working class were becoming less ready to accept humiliating social distinctions.

The best known of the means by which social distinctions were maintained within the church was the system of pew-rents. This was very widely used throughout the nineteenth century, even by the most proletarian denominations such as the Primitive Methodists. In itself it need not have been offensive. But the problems arose when there were sharp gradations in rents, with associated differentials in the quality of seating, or when no free seats were provided for those unable to pay. In the early nineteenth century, some churches were deliberately attracting the rich by excluding the poor, and others were achieving the same result without necessarily intending it. In Glasgow, for instance, fierce interdenominational competition in the later eighteenth century meant that both Establishment and Dissenters courted the middle-class public, whose bulging wallets promised financial salvation. The middle class could be attracted by providing well-known preachers and luxuriously appointed buildings. But all this meant money, which was usually raised by increasing seat-rents. Up until about 1810, prices of more expensive seats were increased, while rents for the inferior seats at the back were frozen. But about that time, the City Council, which owned the Established churches, began to raise rents on the poorer seats as well, or to abolish free and low-rent seating altogether. New churches began to be built specifically for the middle class, and at the Tron church, where the rich tended to come in the morning and the poor in the evening, the former began to complain that the latter were a health hazard. Thus the policy came to be the building of separate purpose-built working-class churches in the poorer parts of the city. However, lack of money for this purpose meant that church-building in the poor east always lagged far behind that in the affluent west [Brown, 1981, I, *311-37*]

Thus in the early years of the nineteenth century poorer members of affluent congregations were being priced out, frozen out, or goaded into leaving by sermons extolling the British Constitution. The atmosphere of these years was well conveyed by a Scottish weaver, writing in 1845 and remembering his days in an Aberdeen factory: 'Had one of us been bold enough to enter a church, he must have been ejected for the sake of decency. His forlorn and curiously patched habilements would have contested the point of attraction with the ordinary eloquence of that period. So for all parties it was better that he kept to the garret, or wandered far "in the deep green wood" ' [W. Thom, *Rhymes and Recollection of a Handloom Weaver*, 1847]. And his assessment of the attitude of the church-goers may not have been far wrong, as in 1849 a parish missionary in that city was privately questioning the genuineness of the conversions of those new members who had failed to prosper after joining the congregation [MacLaren, 1974, *182*].

Organised Christianity in nineteenth-century Britain tended to be a religion of the successful, in which material rewards were expected to follow from Christian living. At one extreme of the scale this could lead to the self-satisfaction of the self-made industrialist, who believed that his wealth was a God-given reward. But many working-class church-goers expected more modest prosperity to follow their conversion. As Durham Methodists around the end of the century put it, Jesus could turn beer into clothes for your children and furniture for your home [Moore, 1974, *142*]. Wesley himself had noted the material benefits that often followed conversion, though he deplored the worldliness that frequently resulted. The corollary drawn by many people (though not by Wesley) was that poverty was a result of sin, and a reason for shame. Therefore the proud poor were likely to shrink from appearing at church. Indeed they might well feel bitterness towards God for having unjustly punished them with poverty.

MacLaren [1974, Chapter 6] has suggested a further, and related, reason for working-class alienation from the Scottish Presbyterian churches in the middle decades of the nineteenth century: middle-class bias in the exercise of church discipline. The Church of Scotland, and most Dissenting denominations in England, Wales and Scotland alike, had strict systems of internal discipline, though these were tending to be relaxed somewhat in the later part of the nineteenth century. His research on Aberdeen between about 1840 and 1865 suggested that the kirk sessions were mainly concerned with punishing drunkenness and sexual offences. In doing this they dealt severely with working-class members, while tending to overlook the misdeeds of those with 'socio-economic status in the community, and who lived in respectable residential areas', unless they held church office, in which case a stricter view could not be avoided. The only typically middle-class offence that kirk sessions frequently dealt with was bankruptcy, and here they were severe, communion usully being denied until the bankrupt had paid his creditors in full. He concludes that 'Church membership to the Victorian businessman was in many ways a mark of his continuing financial stability and social respectability', but that 'no such positive advantages were attached to working class membership', while there was always the risk of 'humiliation and disgrace' at the hands of the kirk sessions. However, MacLaren's conclusions on a wide range of issues, this included, have been challenged by Hillis [1981, 57-64], who has analysed similar records from Glasgow during the same period. He confirms MacLaren's finding that membership of the kirk sessions was heavily middle class, but he finds no evidence of discriminatory application of discipline. Neither did he find much evidence of penalties for bankruptcy. He found that the Established Church concentrated mainly on sexual offences, but showed no regard for social status in punishing them. The Dissenters spread their net more widely, also attacking drunkenness, Sabbath-breaking and failure to attend church. Here, indeed, the poorer working class were more likely to be hit, as they did attend church less than middle-class people, and if they got drunk or broke the Sabbath, they were more likely to do it in a public place, where the offence could be observed and reported.

Thus MacLaren's suggestion that church discipline bore particularly hard on poorer members receives partial corroboration, though Hillis would distinguish more sharply than MacLaren between the more prosperous and the poorer sections of the working class. Certainly there is plenty of evidence that the position of the latter was particularly tenuous, even in the more plebeian denominations, or in those parish churches which retained a more homely atmosphere. The first half of the nineteenth century had seen a proliferation of evangelical movements with a mainly working-class membership, and by the middle of the century the élite-led churches were generally making determined efforts to attract working-class people. But descriptions of working-class congregations repeatedly stressed the atmosphere of respectability and relative prosperity. A typical comment was this by a Sheffield journalist, who toured city churches, and who visited a Congregational chapel in 1873: 'The working classes of Attercliffe who wend their way to Zion must be of a superior class. They looked intelligent and serious, with every indication of attending carefully their inner and outer man ... good trade and high wages muct have been utilised to some purpose of late years' [Wickham, 1957, 136]. Many working-class church-goers agreed in regarding themselves as a superior stratum. Here are extracts from a letter by a Nantyglo miner, written to a Merthyr paper in 1885. He

61

divided the working class into 'the residuum', sunk in 'apathy and indifference', the 'pothouse politicians', and

> another section of the working class. You will find them occupying positions of trust in our iron and tinplate works; superintendents and officials in our Sunday Schools and Non-conformist Churches, presidents of our Temperance Societies and Bands of Hope; leading men in our giant Friendly Society organisation, and led by those champions of civil and religious liberty, the Nonconformist ministry, this section of the working class are exerting an influence upon working class political thought that no-one knows but those who mingle with them. [Lambert, 1976, *6*]

The first comment came at the end of the greatest boom period of the nineteenth century; the second came from a time when south Wales Nonconformity was at the peak of its prosperity, and wide sections of the population had become absorbed into a common Nonconformist-Liberal culture. But even in the 1830s, when working-class prosperity was a rare commodity, there is evidence that churches and chapels attracted the less impoverished, and that in times of acute depression the poorest members tended to drop out rather than face the shame of being unable to pay subscriptions or wear decent clothes. The Leeds Wesleyans explained their losses in the slump of 1841–2 in these terms, and declining church attendance by Scottish handloom weavers in the 1830s was attributed partly to increasing poverty and partly to disillusionment with their ministers [Greaves, 1968, *112-3*; Withrington, 1970]. In any case, as a Birmingham evangelist pointed out, the very poor had little surplus time or energy to devote to anything beyond merely keeping alive: 'The anxieties of the present life so incessantly occupy and fill the mind that [preaching the gospel] is like overfilling and putting more in that which is already full' [Carrs Lane MSS., Vol. 61, entry for 26 January 1838].

Oral history suggests that many working-class mothers in the years around 1900 had no interests outside the home, the usual explanation being 'She hadn't the time'. Equally, their husbands often spent all Sunday in a garden or allotment. Such people might turn up at church when they did have time, which usually meant such special occasions as the Sunday School Anniversary. But there was more open conflict between the church and the other main centre of Sunday activity, the pub. As the son (born 1904) of a Nottingham hosiery worker put it: 'There was nothing else to do, only chapel or church or public houses, that's about all there was, and – if you went to church or chapel you was a snob, and if you went to pub you was a hail fellow well met' [Thompson and Vigne, interviews, no.222, 40]. Pubs and churches were the most important social centres, and they were alike in the fact that each offered its devotees a sense of belonging to a community of like-minded people (if it did not, they quickly moved somewhere else), and each enabled them to rise above the daily grind, to reflect and recuperate. For working-class women, this aspect of the church was especially important, because there were few alternative public meeting places, and the main choice for them was between involvement in the church, and a social life based entirely on family and neighbourhood.

It would of course be quite wrong to assume that the many women and more men who played little or no part in the week-by-week life of the churches and chapels were irreligious. Attempts to define the religion of the non-church-goer remain highly speculative [see McLeod, 1974, 49-60; Obelkevich, 1976, Chapter 6; Cox, 1982, 90-105]. But it is clear from the diaries of city missionaries that many non-church-goers had their own quite strongly held religious beliefs (often very different from those of the missionaries themselves). Equally the evidence of oral history suggests that few working-class people in later nineteenth and early twentieth-century Britian had a consistently secular view of life.

The outstanding collection of Birmingham missionary diaries, dating from the 1830s and 1840s, has been carefully analysed by Robson [1978]. He suggests that the comments recorded reflect not so much indifference to religion as lack of interest in the kind of religion offered by the missionaries (Calvinism), and the prevalence of a 'popular religion' of a different kind, having closest affinities with Methodism. The features of this 'popular religion' included ecstatic experiences, belief in the power of prayer (especially the prayers of a holy man or woman), rejection of the legalistic morality of the Calvinist missionaries (e.g. their sabbatarianism), trust in the expiatory value of present suffering and consequent repudiation of the threat of hell, a stress on practical Christianity and a lack of interest in correct doctrine. The ecstatic element, so important in the religion of the early nineteenth century, is not much in evidence at the end; neither were there any signs of the desire to be prayed over by a holy person that seems to have been so prevalent in the 1830s and 1840s. But otherwise the points mentioned by Robson are equally apparent in the missionary diaries [see McLeod, 1974, 49-54] and the oral evidence from the end of the century. Analysis of the oral evidence on popular religion, with due regard for such factors as regional differences, has hardly begun [but see brief sections in P. Thompson, 1977, *202-8*, and Roberts, 1976, *62-9*], and our understanding of its meaning in people's lives is limited by the fact that questionnaires have tended to focus on the more formal aspects of religion. But one or two recurrent themes can be identified. One is stress on 'practical Christianity', and a tendency to regard other aspects of religion as superfluous, summed up in the description of a London stevedore and his wife as 'one hundred per cent Christians, but not church-goers' [Thompson and Vigne interviews, no. 70, *16*]. Linked with this was an ambivalent attitude towards clergymen and active church-goers: both were bitterly denounced as hypocrites if they showed human imperfections, but greatly admired if they were 'real Christians', which included such qualities as simple living, strict honesty, generosity, and treating everyone alike. Thus a 'good vicar' could enjoy a following extending well beyond the circle of regular church-goers, and a working-class leader, such as George Lansbury, who was regarded as a model Christian, could be revered as 'St George' by many who did not share his devout Anglicanism [cf. Richman, 1976]. Two points that are apparent in a number of Elizabeth Roberts' interviews with working-class women from north Lancashire are the importance of prayer as a source of renewed strength, and a certain fatalism, according to which quite a wide range of things were felt to be the will of God, and any attempt at human interference was discountenanced: this was an effective way of coming to terms with disasters that could not be helped, but it also could mean refusing to take precautions against avoidable disasters (e.g. by practising contraception) [cf. Elizabeth Roberts' interviews with Mrs C3P, *3, 8,* Mrs H4P, Mrs P1P, *12*].

In spite of the fact that many working-class people took little part in church life, the churches were throughout the nineteenth century powerful institutions, impinging on the lives of most of the population in one way or another. The fact that the élite in both town and countryside tended to be strongly identified with one or other of the churches meant that they used their influence to further the interests of their church, and their church to further their own interests; the Established Churches still possessed wide-ranging social functions, inherited from the old regime, and the Dissenters tended to enter into competition with the declining, but still powerful, Establishments; moreover, the churches repeatedly acted as pioneers in the meeting of newly recognised social needs, which no secular agency was yet ready to provide for. To give some examples: MacLaren showed [1974, *126*] that in 1837, 92 per cent of the population of Aberdeen claimed membership of a church, although many of them never attended it. He explained this in terms of the important social services provided by the churches, notably their major role in the provision of schooling, the part played by the kirk session in the distribution of charity, and the advantages of the support of a minister on such occasions as admission to the Infirmary. And Cox argued [1982, *58-9, 85-9*] that by the 1880s 'charity and social services' appeared to be the main *raison d'être* both of Anglican and of Nonconformist churches in south London. He mentions the same points as MacLaren and notes a major new function assumed by many churches towards the end of the nineteenth century: that of providers of cheap entertainment.

However, between about 1880 and 1930 there was a gradual weakening of the position of social influence enjoyed by the churches. One fundamental factor was declining interest in religion on the part of the rich and powerful. Another was the rise of labour from the 1880s on, but more especially after the First World War, leading to a polarisation of politics on class lines; sectarian identity, which had been highly relevant to the politics of the mid-Victorian period, became an increasingly minor factor in most parts of Britain. The paternalist family firms that had dominated so many small towns, and whole districts of major cities, and which often had worked in close co-operation with a church or chapel, were tending to become absorbed into giant combines, with head offices in London. This meant that the employer who met his workers at church, or who showered local places of worship with lavish gifts, became a rarity [Joyce, 1980, *339-40*]. The social services provided by the churches were also declining in importance in this period, partly because of the expanding powers of local and central government [cf. Cox, 1982, Chapter 6], partly because of the rise of the leisure industry. For much of the nineteenth century, churches and chapels had been the main providers of 'respectable' alternative amusements to those provided by public houses. But by the end of the century an increasingly wide range of alternatives was available: professional sport, cycling, music-halls in purpose-built theatres. However, it was only with the radio and the beginnings of the cinema craze in the 1920s that the churches' functions as providers of cheap amusement were essentially superseded, and the gradual relaxation of the restrictions on Sunday leisure continued long beyond the Second World War.

Thus between about 1880 and 1930 new patterns of life were emerging in most parts of Britain, as a result of which, regardless of individual religious belief, the social importance of the churches had greatly diminished. The many extrinsic factors that had increased church membership and attendance for much of the nineteenth century had largely disappeared, and the churches were forced to rely on the intrinsic attractions of their message and of the fellowship they offered. With the slow spread of agnosticism in the early twentieth century, especially under the influence of Robert Blatchford's *God and my Neighbour* (1904), Christianity faced serious ideological competition. Some politically active working-class people constructed a complete alternative world view based on socialism and Darwinism. As a systematic view of life, Christianity in its various forms remained far more popular than any alternative. But more common was a fluid eclecticism, which owed total allegiance to no single religion or ideology.

One important impediment to working-class church-going was in fact being removed in the early twentieth century: smaller families meant that fewer women were perpetually tied to the kitchen. But where the mother of six in 1880 had gratefully seized the opportunity of escaping from home to an occasional Mother's Meeting, the mother of one in 1930 found a much wider range of commercial operators competing for her increased leisure time. Meanwhile, the garden, which had rivalled the pub as a Sunday Mecca for the non-church-going male in the nineteenth century, was becoming more important as more people moved from city-centre slums to council estates with gardens. In the second quarter of the twentieth century the quiet Sunday was becoming even quieter: the sound of hymn-singing grew fainter, but the roar of motor cars had not yet taken its place. For millions of working-class families it was a day for digging the garden, visiting relatives, or snoozing over the *News of the World*.

# Select Bibliography

SECTION I: PRIMARY SOURCES

Here are a few examples of outstanding sources.

Booth Collection, London School of Economics Library. Includes the notebooks filled by Charles Booth during research in the 1890s for his 7-volume work on religion in London.

Carrs Lane Church: Town Mission Journals, Nonconformist Collection, Birmingham Reference Library. An outstanding collection of diaries kept by door-to-door evangelists operating in Birmingham in the 1830s and 1840s.

Chester Diocesan Articles of Enquiry, 1778–1825, Cheshire County Record Office. Fascinating reports by clergy from Industrial Revolution Lancashire.

Lawson, J., *Letters to the Young on Progress in Pudsey during the last Sixty Years* (Stanningley, 1887). Offers many novel perspectives on social change in the nineteenth century.

Mann, Horace, Religious Census of 1851. Results published in *Parliamentary Papers*, 1852–3, vol. LXXXIX (England & Wales), 1854, Vol. LIX (Scotland).

Roberts, Elizabeth, Oral History of Working Class in Barrow, Lancaster and Preston. Indexed transcripts of 170 interviews relating to 1890–1930, at Centre for North-West Regional Studies, University of Lancaster.

Thompson, Paul and Vigne, Thea, Interviews on Family Life and Work Experience before 1918. Tapes and transcripts at Department of Sociology, University of Essex.


SECTION II: HISTORICAL STUDIES

Ainsworth, A., 'Religion in the Working Class Community and the Evolution of Socialism in later Nineteenth Century Lancashire', *Historie Sociale*, X (1977). A useful critique of many received ideas.

Baxter, J., 'The Great Yorkshire Revival, 1792–6', in M. Hill (ed.),

*Sociological Yearbook of Religion in Britain*, 7 (1974). Detailed local evidence in support of E. P. Thompson's interpretation of Methodism.

Billington, L., 'Popular Religion and Social Reform: A Study of Teetotalism and Revivalism, 1830–50', *Journal of Religious History*, X (1978–9).

Brown, C. G., 'Religion and the Development of an Urban Society: Glasgow, 1780–1914', Ph.D. thesis, University of Glasgow (1981). The most ambitious contribution yet made to the social history of modern Scottish religion.

Budd, S., *Varieties of Unbelief* (1977). A comprehensive history of the secular and humanist movements.

Campbell, A. B., *The Lanarkshire Miners: A Social History of their Trade Unions, 1775-1874* (Edinburgh, 1979). Useful on sectarianism.

Colls, R., *The Collier's Rant* (1977). Includes lively discussion of north-eastern Methodism.

Cox, J., *The English Churches in a Secular Society: Lambeth, 1870-1930* (Oxford, 1982). A provocative interpretation of church decline.

Davies, E. T., *Religion in the Industrial Revolution in South Wales* (Cardiff, 1965). The best synthesis.

Davies, R., George, A. R. and Rupp, G., *A History of the Methodist Church in Great Britain*, Vol. II (1978).

Dews, D. C. (ed.), *From Mow Cop to Peake*, Wesley Historical Society, Yorkshire branch, Occasional Paper no. 4 (Leeds, 1982). Useful essays on Primitive Methodism.

Drummond, A. L. and Bulloch, J., *The Church in late Victorian Scotland, 1874-1900* (Edinburgh, 1978). Final volume of a useful series on Scottish church history.

Dyos, H. J. and Wolff, M. (eds), *The Victorian City*, Vol. II (1973). Good sections on religion.

Evans, D. G., 'The Growth and Development of Organised Religion in the Swansea Valley, 1820–1890', Ph.D. thesis, University of Wales (1977). Criticises Davies' rather negative treatment of Nonconformity.

Faulkner, H. U., *Chartism and the Churches* (New York, 1916).

Field, C. D., 'The Social Structure of English Methodism, Eighteenth-Twentieth Centuries,' *British Journal of Sociology*, XXVIII (1977). Thorough analysis of statistical evidence.

Foster, J., *Class Struggle and the Industrial Revolution* (1974). An important study, though treatment of religion is rather thin.

Gilbert, A. D., *Religion and Society in Industrial England, 1740-1914*

*(1976)*. A major synthesis.

Gilbert, A. D., 'Methodism, Dissent and political stability in early Industrial England', *Journal of Religious History*, X (1978–9). An important contribution to the 'Methodism and Revolution' debate.

Greaves, B., 'Methodism in Yorkshire, 1740–1851', Ph.D. thesis, University of Liverpool (1968).

Harrison, B., 'Religion and Recreation in Nineteenth-Century England', *Past & Present*, no. 38 (1967).

Harrison, J. F. C., *The Second Coming* (1979). Best book on modern British millenarians.

Hillis, P., 'Presbyterianism and Social Class in mid-Nineteenth-Century Glasgow: A Study of nine Churches', *Journal of Ecclesiastical History*, XXXII (1981). Uses statistical evidence to challenge MacLaren.

Hobsbawm, E. J., *Labouring Men* (1964). Includes a significant contribution to debate on Methodism.

Hobsbawm, E. J., *Primitive Rebels* (2nd edn, Manchester, 1971). Interesting discussion of role of religion in working-class political movements.

Hopkins, E., 'Religious Dissent in Black Country Industrial Villages in the first Half of the Nineteenth Century,' *Journal of Ecclesiastical History*, XXXIV (1983).

Hopkins, J. K., *A Woman to Deliver her People: Joanna Southcott and English Millenarianism in an Era of Revolution* (Austin, 1982).

Inglis, K. S., *Churches and the Working Classes in Victorian England* (1963). Stimulating study of church responses to working-class irreligion.

Jones, P. d'A., *The Christian Socialist Revival, 1877-1914* (Princeton, 1968).

Jones, R. M., *The North Wales Quarrymen, 1874-1922* (Cardiff, 1981).

Joyce, P., *Work, Society and Politics* (Brighton, 1980). Like Foster's book, a major reinterpretation of nineteenth-century Lancashire history. Relates religion to factory paternalism and to ethnic conflict.

Kendall, H. B., *History of the Primitive Methodist Connexion* (1902). Not yet entirely superseded.

Kent, J., *Holding the Fort* (1978). A stimulating study of revivalism.

Lambert, W. R., 'Some Working-Class Attitudes towards organised Religion in Nineteenth-Century Wales', *Llafur*, II (1976).

Laqueur, T. W., *Religion and Respectability: Sunday Schools and Working Class Culture, 1780-1850* (New Haven, 1976). An important critique of E. P. Thompson's interpretation of early nineteenth-century religion.

Lees, L. H., *Exiles of Erin: Irish Immigrants in Victorian London* (Manchester, 1979).

Lunn, K. (ed.), *Hosts, Immigrants and Minorities* (Folkestone, 1980). Useful sections on Catholicism and anti-Catholicism in Lancashire and Glasgow.

MacLaren, A. A., *Religion and Social Class: The Disruption Years in Aberdeen* (1974). An important study, focused mainly on middle class.

McLeod, H., 'Class, Community and Region: The Religious Geography of Nineteenth-Century England', M. Hill (ed.), *Sociological Yearbook of Religion in Britain, 6* (1973).

McLeod, H., *Class and Religion in the late Victorian City* (1974). London, c.1880–1914.

McLeod, H., *Religion and the People of Western Europe, 1789-1970* (Oxford, 1981).

Meacham, S., *A Life Apart* (1977). Working-class neighbourhood life, c.1890–1914. Minimises role of religion.

Moore, R., *Pit-men, Politics and Preachers* (1974). Excellent study of relationship between religion and politics in Durham mining villages.

Morgan, K. O., *Keir Hardie* (1975).

Morgan, K. O., *Rebirth of a Nation: Wales 1880-1980* (Oxford, 1981).

Obelkevich, J., *Religion and Rural Society: South Lindsey, 1825-75* (Oxford, 1976). A classic study, which raises many questions about urban religion.

Pelling, H., *Social Geography of British Elections, 1885-1910* (1967). Includes many references to the influence of religion.

Pelling, H., *Popular Politics and Society in late Victorian Britain* (1968)

Phillips, P. T., *The Sectarian Spirit: Sectarianism, Society and Politics in Victorian Cotton Towns* (Toronto, 1982).

Richman, G., *Fly a Flag for Poplar* (1976). Oral history of East London.

Roberts, E., *Working Class Barrow and Lancaster, 1890-1930* (Lancaster, 1976).

Robson, G., 'The Failures of Success: Working Class Evangelists in early Victorian Birmingham,' D. Baker (ed.) *Religious Motivation*, Studies in Church History, XV (Oxford, 1978).

Robson, G., 'Between Town and Country: Contrasting Patterns of Churchgoing in the early Victorian Black Country', D. Baker (ed.),

*The Church in Town and Country*, Studies in Church History, XVI (Oxford, 1979).

Rose, E. A., *Methodism in Droylesden, 1776-1963* (n.p., n.d.). One of a useful series on Lancashire and Cheshire Methodism.

Royle, E., *Victorian Infidels* (Manchester, 1974).

Royle, E., *Radicals, Secularists and Republicans: Popular Free Thought in Britain, 1866-1915* (Manchester, 1980).

Rule, J., 'The Labouring Miner in Cornwall, *c.*1740-1870', Ph.D. thesis, University of Warwick, 1971.

Shallice, A., 'Orange and Green and militancy: Sectarianism and Working Class Politics in Liverpool, 1900-14', *North West Labour History Society Bulletin. 6* (1979-1980)

Shiels, W. J. (ed.), *The Church and Healing*, Studies in Church History, XIX (Oxford, 1982). Includes novel insights into nineteenth-century popular religion.

Stigant, P., 'Wesleyan Methodism and Working Class Radicalism in the North, 1792-1821', *Northern History*, VI (1971)

Summers, D. F., 'The Labour Church and allied Movements of the late Nineteenth and early Twentieth Centuries', Ph.D. thesis, University of Edinburgh, 1958. A fascinating reconstruction, drawing heavily on the memories of survivors.

Thompson, E. P., *The Making of the English Working Class* (2nd edn, Harmondsworth, 1968). Essential reading for all aspects of English history *c.*1790-1830.

Thompson, P., *The Edwardians* (1977). Draws heavily on oral evidence.

Valenze, D., 'Prophetic Sons and Daughters: Popular Religion and Social Change in England, 1790-1850', Ph.D. thesis, Brandeis University, 1982. Mainly about Primitive Methodist women.

Walker, W. M., *Juteopolis: Dundee's Textile Workers, 1885-1923* (Edinburgh, 1979). Includes novel perspectives on their religion.

Wallace, C. I., 'Religion and Society in Eighteenth Century England: Geographic, Demographic and Occupational Patterns of Dissent in the West Riding of Yorkshire', Ph.D. thesis, Duke University, 1975.

Waller, P. J., *Democracy and Sectarianism: A Political and Social History of Liverpool, 1868-1939* (Liverpool, 1981).

Ward, W. R., *Religion and Society in England, 1790-1850* (1972). A stimulating interpretation. *Not* an introduction.

Wearmouth, R. F., *Methodism and the Working Class Movements of England, 1800-50* (1937). Part of a series intended to document and vindicate the role of Methodists in the labour movement.

Wickham, E. R., *Church and People in an Industrial City* (1957). Pioneering study of Sheffield.

Wilson, A., *Scottish Chartism* (Manchester, 1970).

Withrington, D., 'Non-Church-Going in Scotland, *c.*1750–1850: A preliminary Survey', *Records of the Scottish Church History Society*, XVII (1970).

Yeo, E., 'Christianity in Chartist Struggle, 1838–42,' *Past & Present*, no. 91 (1981). A valuable reinterpretation.

Yeo, S., *Religion and Voluntary Organisations in Crisis* (1976). Important study of churches in Reading, *c.*1890–1914.

Yeo, S., 'A New Life: The Religion of Socialism in Britain, 1883–96', *History Workshop Journal*, no. 4 (1977).

# Index

Established churches  17–18,  22,  36,
    39–43, 57–8, 64–5
Evangelical Union  35

factory workers  22–3, 24, 31, 32, 41–
    2, 52, 59–60
Foster, John  31–2
Free Church of Scotland  12, 42, 44
French Revolution  18–19

Gilbert, A. D.  23–5, 30–2, 50–2
Glasgow  14, 37–8, 45, 48, 55, 59, 61
Glasgow Celtic FC  16
Glasse, Rev. J.  45
Good Templars  35

Haldane brothers  21
Halifax  51
Hardie, Keir  35
Hartley, Sir William  30
Headlam, Rev. S.  45
Hillis, P.  61
Hobsbawm, E. J.  23, 51–2
home missions  10, 16, 60, 63
Horner, Arthur  55–6
Huddersfield  23
Hyde  49

Independents  see Congregationalists
Independent Labour Party  45, 54, 55
Independent Methodists  46
indifference, religious  9, 10, 11, 17–18,
    20–1, 24, 31, 57–8
industrial villages  13, 17–18, 22–3, 24,
    53
Inglis, K. S.  11, 12, 15
Invernessshire  58
Irish in Britain  12, 37–9

Jowett, F.  48
Joyce, Patrick  31–2, 52–3

Keighley  47
Kendall, H. B.  28, 29–30
Kent, John  52

Labour churches  48–9
Labour Party  43, 44–5, 54, 55
Lanarkshire  35, 42

Lancashire  10, 14, 17, 20–1, 30, 31–2,
    37–8, 41, 46, 47, 52, 54, 64
Lansbury, George  64
Laqueur, T. W.  23
Leeds  17, 62
Leicester  13
Liberal Party  43, 44–5, 54
Lincolnshire  25
Liverpool  13, 37–8, 42
London  13, 14, 18, 19, 20, 45, 64, 65
Loughborough  29
lower middle class  22, 31, 33, 39, 40
Ludlam, Isaac  51

MacLaren, A. A.  12, 15, 60–1, 65
magic  25, 27, 33
Magic Methodists  26
Manchester  18, 20, 47, 48
Mann, Horace  57
Marx, Karl  22
Marxism  9, 49, 54–6
Maurice, Rev. F. D.  54
Meacham, Standish  11, 12
men, in relation to churches  14, 27–8,
    62–3
Merthyr Tydfil  13, 61–2
Methodists  9, 14, 16, 17, 21–5, 29, 32,
    34, 45–6, 49–53, 62
    see also  Bible Christians, Calvinistic
    Methodists,  Independent  Method-
    ists,  Magic  Methodists,  Primitive
    Methodists,  Wesleyans,  Wesleyan
    Reformers
Methodist New Connexion  19, 46, 51
Methodist Unitarians  46–7
Miall, Rev. E.  44
middle class  9, 12, 14, 15, 16, 17, 30,
    31, 54, 57, 58–61, 64–5
millenarianism  19
miners  12, 13, 14, 17, 28–9, 35, 42
ministers of religion  9, 11, 44–6, 57–8
    Anglican  17, 18, 20–1, 24, 28, 36,
    38, 44–5, 64
    Nonconformist  31, 44–6, 48, 50–1,
    62
    Roman Catholic  38–9, 46, 55
    Scottish  17, 18, 35, 36, 44–6, 48, 65
    lay preachers  21, 46, 51, 54–5
    women preachers  27–8, 30

of new chapels   21
Stephenson, William   51
Stigant, P.   25
Stockport   49
strikes   28, 42, 54
subcultures
   Catholic   39
   radical   20
   socialist   52
Sunday   20, 49, 62–3, 66
Swedenborgians   47

textile workers   17–18, 20–1, 24, 31, 34, 59–60
Thompson, E. P.   9, 11, 22–3, 25, 29, 50–1, 54
Thompson, Paul   10, 14, 15, 34, 42–3
Tolstoy, L.   54
Tories   *see* Conservative
trade unions   22, 28, 35, 39, 42, 52–3, 54
Trevor, Rev. J.   48

Unitarians   46–7, 48, 49
United Presbyterians   44
urbanisation   22, 23, 24, 30–1

Valenze, Deborah   27, 29
Vigne, Thea   10, 14, 15, 34, 42–3

Wales   12, 13, 21–2, 41, 42, 44, 57, 60
   north   42, 58
   south   12, 43, 54–6, 62
Warrington   46
Wearmouth, R. F.   9, 25, 50
Wesley, Rev. J.   17, 50, 60
Wesleyan Methodists   14, 19, 26, 27, 32, 34, 46, 50–2, 62
Wesleyan Reformers   51
Wheatley, John   55
Whigs   29, 44, 51
Whit Walks   41
Wickham, E. R.   9, 11, 12, 15, 31–2
Wilson, John,   52–3
Wiltshire   27
Wise, Pastor G.   38
women, in relation to churches   14, 15, 27–8, 29, 30, 33, 34, 46, 62–4, 66

Yeo, Eileen   51
York   51
Yorkshire   14, 19, 21, 24, 30, 34, 43, 46, 47, 54